D1568759

LUST
The Other Side of Love

LUST

The Other Side of Love

Mel White

Fleming H. Revell Company
Old Tappan, New Jersey

CONTENTS

ACKNOWLEDGMENTS

Thank you, Lyla, for your love, your trust, your patience, and your good humor during this last long year of LUST.

Thank you, Erin and Michael, for not letting my closed door and fierce scowls keep you from interrupting me. You two are more important to me than all the books, films, and sermons put together.

Thank you, Bill and Hugh Barbour, Richard Baltzell, Ernie Owen, Bruce Barbour, Astrid Seeburg, Ann Curtiss, Evelyn Sendecke, and all my other friends at Fleming H. Revell Company for suggesting this book and for helping each step along the way.

Thank you, all my friends who read and critiqued the rough manuscript and made so many helpful suggestions.

And thanks to you, Glory, Jeri, Delores, and Gordon, for typing and Xeroxing the manuscript.

FOREWORD
A Little Story

A long time ago, in Santa Cruz, a beach town on the bay, a twelve-year-old boy and girl met and became friends. They spent many hours walking together and talking about school, growing up, and God. They read their awkward poems to each other, chased crabs among the rocks, and swam in the sea.

The boy was a Christian, and by the time they were into their senior year of high school, the girl came to an understanding of his faith and accepted Jesus as her Lord and Saviour.

In college they dated and fell in love. Although it was difficult to wait, they didn't marry until after graduation. Then they sailed on the *Queen Elizabeth* for a four-month honeymoon, making love in romantic places in Europe and the Near East. They learned many exciting things about the world and about each other.

In time, they finished graduate school. She taught English literature. He produced films, taught in a seminary, and pastored a city church. They wrote books together. They bought a little house and had two children whose presence brought much pleasure and delight. One might say they lived happily ever after—except that in real life no one really lives happily ever after. Life brought this couple tragedies and tears as well as adventures and joy.

But they shared their fears and tears. They encouraged each other to take risks. They had many happy moments and much laughter. Now they look back at their fifteen years of marriage and say, "It has been very good."

Then one summer the man decided to write a book about lust. They both thought the book might help people. When friends and neighbors heard about his project, they said to the woman, "How do you feel about this book? Isn't it threatening? What if people misunderstand?" But the woman only smiled and said, "Those who love and enjoy and trust each other know that the other side of lust is love."

LYLA WHITE

Introduction

PRESIDENT CARTER, YOU, AND ME
(Do I Lust?)

On July 21, 1976, Presidential Candidate Jimmy Carter stood on the front steps of his home in Plains, Georgia, and confessed his struggle with sexual lust to reporters:

> I've looked on a lot of women with lust. I've committed adultery in my heart many times. This is something that God recognizes I will do—and I have done it—and God forgives me for it.

Carter's confession was published in *Playboy* magazine (September 20, 1976) and made banner headlines around the world. People rushed to respond . . . .

"Lust Is a Silly, Outdated Notion"

Millions of people snickered or laughed out loud at this Baptist layman's confession. They grinned in disbelief that a national figure could still believe that thinking about sexual intercourse with anyone except his wife could be wrong or need God's forgiveness. Jimmy Carter's Sunday-school notions seemed very out of touch with current sexual standards. Our culture calls us to feel anything but guilt. "Sex is a natural appetite. When you get hungry, feed it!"

Few of those who laughed off Carter's confession bothered to count the cost of our new sexual freedom. Between 1963 and 1975 the divorce rate doubled. Serious sex crimes involving incest, rape, and child molestation are epidemic. Venereal disease is rampant in junior-high and elementary-school children. Court-appointed psychologists are uncovering sexual lust as a primary factor in a growing number of assaults, kidnapings, and murders, and in other violent crimes against persons.

Jimmy Carter's confession made a lot of people laugh. But his words reminded all of us that for four thousand years our Hebrew-Christian tradition has consistently warned us against the results of "doing what comes naturally" without ethical guidelines and restraints. Bible stories tell in lurid detail the horror and heartbreak of runaway sexual lust. The collected wisdom of two thousand years of biblical history from Abraham to Jesus confronts our modern sexual standards and confirms our fears that sexual lust is not a silly, outdated notion. Lust is an evil force working to destroy individuals, families, cities, and nations. And the louder we laugh at another man's confession, the more we show our own weakness and vulnerability.

"Lust Is Something We Don't Talk About"

Others responded in shock and surprise at Mr. Carter's openness. They reminded him that sexual lust is something a Christian is not supposed to talk about, at least not in public. "Imagine the risk you take in making such a confession," thought his critics. "It may damage your Christian witness." "It may hurt your public career or embarrass your family and friends." "It may cause people to feel uneasy around you. Worse, it will make you more vulnerable to those who know your weakness and take unfair advantage of it.''

From childhood we have learned to wear masks to cover up much of what we think, feel, or act sexually. No pastor or teacher, no well-meaning parent or friend intended to force us into secrecy and silence. They just passed on to us what they learned from their own pastor or teacher, from their well-meaning parent or friend. The resulting silence has been disastrous.

For example, one young, unmarried man was told that masturbation was a terrible sin. Someone quoted Genesis 38:9 to him. (The verse concerns a man who refused to impregnate his brother's widow as required by ancient Hebrew laws and ''spilled his seed on the ground'' instead. His sin was not in masturbation, but in refusing to obey God and to create heirs for his dead brother.) The sensitive, talented boy, a victim of this misused Bible story and our unwritten code of silence, could not live with his growing guilt about masturbation.

One night he acted out his misunderstanding of another biblical text: ''If your hand offend you, cut it off.'' (Jesus told this parable to illustrate the seriousness of our struggle with evil, not as a piece of literal advice to a young man troubled by masturbation.) But up against our wall of silence, feeling guilty and alone, the young man emasculated himself with a razor. Our silence drove him to that tragic, destructive act.

Why should we be secretive about sex when biblical writers speak with amazing and helpful frankness? Why should we hide our sexual struggles from each other when we can read in the Bible frank details of the sexual struggles of the great men and women of Scripture? Why should we go on being silent when it causes so many of our brothers and sisters such great suffering?

"Lust Has Easy Answers"

A third way people responded to Carter's confession was by assuring him that Christians don't need to struggle with sexual lust. They wrote to recommend certain Christian disciplines or deeper life experiences that would remove the struggle with sexual lust forever. Others simply promised to pray that Mr. Carter would find victory in his life over this terrible sin and predicted that if his faith were strong enough, God would grant him "a miracle of deliverance."

One Saturday night I saw a black-toupeed, tuxedo-jacketed television healer with his arm outstretched above a crowd of believers. Suddenly he shouted to them, "Praise God! Someone out there in videoland has been healed of sexual lust." I believe in miracles. I am convinced that God is still alive and working in our lives. But after a steady diet of religious books, television programs, and films featuring quick, easy answers and guaranteed, pat solutions, I am afraid that we may forget that miracles are the exception and not the rule. That's one reason they are called miracles. In Christ there are answers to sexual lust, but they are not easy answers.

We are sexual beings from our birth until our death. Every new stage along the way means new questions, new disciplines, new opportunity for sexual wholeness or sexual lust. We need to get down to the serious business of understanding, enjoying and controlling our sexuality as God planned it. God did not use miracles to rescue Samson, David, Solomon, and countless other great men and women of Scripture from their lust. There will probably be no easy miracles for us.

What Is Lust?

I am grateful for Mr. Carter's confession and the loud confusion that followed it. His honesty almost cost him the election, but it got me started on a serious quest for what the Bible teaches about lust. Because I, too, am an evangelical Christian and because I, too, struggle with temptation, my search for practical biblical guidelines was long overdue.

Looking over samples of the letters and telegrams mailed in response to Mr. Carter's confession makes it clear that *lust* is a dangerous word to use, let alone to confess. It creates all kinds of different X-rated pictures for those who hear it. There is no common definition.

The ten-pound *Random House Dictionary* defines lust as "sexual desire or appetite." That definition seems far too all-inclusive for me. Sexual desire or appetite is natural, right, and God-given. To be aroused by a beautiful body is part of the life process as God designed it. For Mr. Carter, sexual lust was not just "sexual arousal" but *runaway, uncontrolled* sexual arousal. He said, "I've committed adultery in my heart many times." Lust was not simply being aroused by a beautiful woman. Lust was allowing that arousal process to continue until he had imagined sexual intercourse with the object of his arousal.

It is interesting to note that, in the context of *Playboy* magazine, Mr. Carter does not pause to defend his assumption that adultery is wrong. The first reason for his belief is safe to assume. Given Mr. Carter's evangelical Christian background, he finds adultery to be wrong because God's Word says it is wrong. The Bible is clear. To commit adultery (intercourse with someone other than your husband or wife) is disobedient and dishonoring to God. But true stories in the ancient text itself give a second reason underlying the first—one that Mr. Carter's years of service as a deacon in his local Baptist church have certainly confirmed. Adultery is wrong because of the painful human damage it so invariably inflicts.

However, adultery is not the only form that lust takes. It seems safe to assume that Mr. Carter used adultery as the only example of lust because beautiful women have been the object of his own personal struggle. For others, the object of lust may be a handsome man, a child, a relative, or a member of their own sex. Therefore, in the stories that follow, when I use the word *lust,* I mean any sexual thought or action that is potentially disobedient or dishonoring to God or potentially demeaning or destructive to people. And when I use the phrase "struggle with lust," I mean those times when we are tempted, when we know the potential for lust in our own lives but are still deciding whether we will give in to lust or resist its pressure.

Notice that I widen the definition of lust to include the action as well as the thought. It is common to define lust as something that happens only in the head. When lust goes on from thought to action, it is usually called only by the action's name, for example: incest, rape, adultery, and the like. I use the term to describe the lust process from thought through action, because lust is the common source of all the different actions, the power that keeps the action going, and the only word we have to describe the entire process.

For Jimmy Carter, lust in the head (the *thought* of adultery) and lust in the flesh (the *act* of adultery) are both *lust* and equally sinful. He quoted Jesus to make his point: "I tell you that anyone who looks on a woman with lust has in his heart already committed adultery."

In Jesus' time, there was, as there is today, an informal popular rating scale to evaluate the seriousness of one's sexual sin. If today the scale were ONE to TEN, child rape would be a TEN. Even convicted murderers in prison will not associate with a child molester. Raping a woman might rate a FIVE or less because of the common rationalization that the victim has somehow helped provoke the attack. Intercourse between consenting unmarried adults of the same sex might get an EIGHT, while adultery or premarital sex might get a ONE rating, if any. "Lust in the head" would get a ZERO. This kind of lust is popularly considered harmless, normal, even necessary.

This is a very misleading scale. Cancer in the body is cancer before it is diagnosed, before the symptoms are noticed, before it has been identified and classified by its type, before the treatment has proven ineffective, and before the obituary notice records another cancer-caused death. Lust, like cancer, is death at work in the body, however early its stage or however "acceptable" its form.

Jesus taught His disciples not to make the dangerous distinction between lust as thought and lust as action. If we see lust only as harmless sexual fantasy, we forget that the worst sexual crimes begin as harmless sexual fantasies in someone's head. By our casual and undisciplined approach to lust in its early thought stages, we miss the opportunity to control lust while control is still possible. By rating another's lust as worse than ours, we may overlook how harmful ours can be. And by our pride we may isolate ourselves from God and from our fellow strugglers when we need them most.

Is Lust a Common Problem?

Mr. Carter said, "I try not to commit a deliberate sin. I recognize that I'm going to do it anyhow, because I am human and I am tempted." Is there any one of us, in spite of our differences in background or belief, who cannot relate at least to this one phrase in Mr. Carter's confession: "I am

human and I am tempted''? When he says, "I am human,"
he seems to be saying, "I have needs." When he says, "I
am tempted," he seems to be saying, "There are times that
I feel pressured to meet those needs in ways that even I
believe are wrong or harmful."

It is easy to guess Mr. Carter's needs as a submarine
commander, locked beneath the sea in a steel tube—or as a
political candidate, locked in to an endless nightmare of
hotel and conference rooms, coffee shops, and all-night
plane rides. He lived under constant pressure, regularly
isolated from wife and family, needing to succeed, facing
enormous risks, often criticized and rejected, taking little
time for rest or recreation, and often bored or restless.
Thereby he was forced to "tough it out," afraid to fail or
confess failure. There was little time, energy, or opportunity for building a creative and fulfilling sexual relationship
in marriage—and few opportunities for intimate friendships. He was thus often alone with his thoughts and fantasies.

Now take Mr. Carter, or any one of us experiencing these
universal human needs, and place him in a world obsessed
with sex. In the cramped quarters of his submarine or in the
airports, hotel rooms, and city centers of the world, he is
surrounded by sexual input: billboards, magazine ads, television programs and commercials, behavior manuals,
plays, films, books, magazines, popular music, bumper
stickers, jokes, clothing styles, display windows, posters,
even printed T-shirts (THIS BODY IS MINE, BUT I SHARE).
Make a list of the things you see in any one day that are
deliberately designed as sexual turn-ons. There is no easy
way to escape our culture's preoccupation with sex: easy
sex, irresponsible sex, sex without commitment, sex to escape the pressure. At the heart of this sexual overload is the

popular lie that sex is an answer for our larger human needs and pressures. Mr. Carter is not the only one who has been tricked by that lie.

I am a pastor and a seminary professor. Seldom does a week pass that I don't discover again that Jimmy Carter's struggle with sexual lust is a common struggle. On Sunday morning my church is full of people, many of whom have attended church and Sunday school all their lives. They represent a cross section of the American church. They are evangelicals. Some are charismatics; some are not. All believe in Christ as Saviour and Lord and see the Bible as the Word of God. Yet I believe that each in his or her own way has been deeply affected by someone's struggle with sexual lust—and that all too many have been damaged to some degree by the church's silence or misunderstanding of this issue.

My students in America's largest independent evangelical seminary come from fifty states and more than two hundred denominations. They are "the best and the brightest" produced by Christian homes and leading American evangelical churches. For ten years I have been a teacher and a counselor among them. My fellow teachers and counselors have confirmed the obvious. Far too many of these young men and women have been deeply affected by the struggle with sexual lust.

Late at night, when my phone rings or a quiet knock is heard at our front door, it is quite probable that in the next few hours someone, clutching a coffee cup in one hand and a wad of Kleenex in the other, will pour out another sad story of lust and its power in his or her life. Over the past fifteen years I have heard firsthand what goes on behind the masks of so many of those Christians who worship and study beside us. Nothing could surprise me anymore.

Whether young or old, rich or poor, beautiful or ugly, married or single, they are affected by a wide range of sexual passions.

As I sit and listen to others confess their struggles to me, I often wonder if those who seek me out as counselor and friend have any idea about my own struggle against sexual lust. People always seem shocked and surprised when I claim that preachers often struggle with lust like everyone else. Later I will be sharing aspects of my own personal struggle with lust and how God helps me in the struggle, but now it is enough to admit that I struggle.

You will probably notice that I never really make clear the object of my sexual lust. Some who read the draft of the manuscript immediately supposed I had had an extramarital affair. Others guessed across the spectrum from a retarded adolescent guilt about masturbation to a closet homosexuality. The object of my lust is not unique, interesting, or important. Really, does it matter how we differ in our sexual desires? If you struggle against adultery or incest, if you struggle against pornography or voyeurism or a pesky fetish, if you struggle against homosexual or bisexual or heterosexual lust, our struggle is the same in the significant ways.

Does Everyone Struggle With Sexual Lust?

You may find it difficult to relate to any of this talk about a struggle with sexual lust. You may experience little if any sexual temptation. You are not abnormal if lust of the sexual variety is not a problem or is no longer a problem. However, for most of us our sexuality, though a source of great joy, is at least an occasional source of struggle as well.

Some people find their sex-related problems few and rather easily managed. For others, sexuality is a lifelong source of pain and frustration, and some may repress their sexual feelings, unable or unwilling to deal with them. Others may be so preoccupied with different struggles that there is neither time nor energy for sexual lust. For instance, drug addicts, alcoholics, compulsive gamblers, workaholics, even religious or political zealots, can get so caught up in what they are doing, that they never relate to sexual temptation. Others give up struggling and give in to failure and guilt or to a series of self-deceptions that deny or laugh away the moral dimensions of their sexuality.

If you are not struggling with lust of the sexual variety, remember that lust may take countless other forms. Temptation comes in as many different varieties as there are people being tempted. We all know temptation. We all know failure. The true stories that follow give us valuable insights into the cause and cure for temptation, whatever form it takes. As you read the accounts of other peoples' triumphs and tragedies, think about your own struggles, sexual or otherwise. Remember that God has no favorite sinner. He has no favored sin. We are all in this together.

Why Confess?

The real problem which Mr. Carter was trying to point out in his confession as quoted in *Playboy* was the problem of pride. He said, "What Christ taught about most was pride, that one person should never think he was any better than anybody else." Mr. Carter went on to relate Jesus' parable of the church leader and the tax collector (as told in Luke 18:9–14). Two men stood praying side-by-side one Sabbath morning. The churchman prayed, "O Lord, I thank Thee that I am not like the rest of men—greedy, dishonest, adulterous." Then he bragged to God about his fasting time and his generous gifts to the synagogue. The

poor tax collector could not even lift his head to heaven, but
beat on his chest in agony, confessing, "O God, have mercy
on me, sinner that I am."

Jesus said it was the tax collector who confessed his sins
who went home pardoned—and not the churchman who
refused to confess. Ken Medema ends his song "Mr.
Simon," a musical version of this story, with these lines:

> Oh, two men walked into the church
> Upon that Sunday morn.
> One left slightly wrinkled,
> The other left reborn.

It may not be easy to confess our failures, but the
confession—or the refusal to confess—has significant,
long-range implications. To confess, even if it is only to
ourselves, can be the beginning step toward forgiveness and
new life. To refuse to confess can have disastrous results
for others and for ourselves. Jesus ended the parable with
this warning: ". . . For everyone who makes himself great
will be humbled, and everyone who humbles himself, will
be made great" (Luke 18:14 TEV).

But Are There Any Solutions?

When Mr. Carter humbled himself to confess his sexual
lust, he became the butt of a million jokes and snide asides
on network talk shows, in locker rooms, and at cocktail
parties across the land. But I am guessing that, in the light
of history, his confession will add to his greatness as a man
and as a Christian. For if taken seriously, his casual confession is a subtle attack on two currently popular but inadequate solutions to our struggle with temptation.

The first lie which his confession confronts is the lie that
there are no moral standards to guide us in our conduct, no

rights and wrongs, no goods or bads. In the sixties we tried this "new," casual, anything-goes morality. Too many people got hurt. The price we paid is still being counted in the rising statistics on suicide, emotional breakdown, drug misuse and addiction, child abuse, incest, adultery and divorce, rape and other sex-related crimes.

Mr. Carter's confession also attacked a second popular though inadequate solution to the struggle with temptation. By admitting his own ongoing struggle with lust, he refused to endorse those of his fellow Christians who—in their zeal to oppose the "new morality"—tend to oversimplify the answer by promising, in rebirth or in a second religious experience, an instant, miraculous end to temptation.

Instead of giving in to the "new morality" or to the miracle cures of popular religion, through his confession Mr. Carter demonstrated God's solution to temptation. That solution began just outside a garden at the beginning of time. It climaxed in the life, death, and resurrection of Jesus of Nazareth. It continues on our behalf today in Christ's Spirit—living and working in His body, the church.

In the following stories from Scripture, we will search for God's answers to the common struggle with lust. The Bible stories are not for children, for they often report in frank, even frightening detail the problems and solutions for lust. At the end of each true-life story, the content is summarized and the biblical references are listed.

Sometimes the Bible answers questions more specifically than we might like. More often the ancient writers leave us with only general guidelines and the freedom to make responsible decisions for ourselves. That is why I have chosen some stories that do not seem to be about sexual lust. But stories about Christ's temptation, about the Holy Spirit, the church, and God's amazing grace *do* pertain significantly to our struggle with sexual lust. I hope that these stories will excite you about going to the Bible and reading them in the original for yourself.

Occasionally I comment on these stories from the perspective of my own struggle with sexual lust. Please forgive these personal references if they are not helpful to you. I have included them for two reasons. First, I did not want to pretend by my silence that I have never been tempted, or that through my Christian experience the temptations miraculously ended, or that one ever grows old enough or wise enough to be above the possibility of facing temptation again. Second, I want to illustrate from the life I know best that the Bible is a helpful, practical, and down-to-earth guide for those who struggle with any kind of temptation.

For thousands of years, men and women facing real temptations, like those we face, have experienced God's solution to their struggle. The Bible is the story of God at work in their lives, guiding them through temptations, forgiving them when they fail, helping them to begin again, teaching them to know and do good, and loving them each step of the slow but certain journey to the victory He has promised.

This book is their story and mine. For—like Adam and Eve, Solomon and the children of Israel, David and Bathsheba, Hosea and Gomer, the adulterous woman of Jerusalem, the incestuous men of Corinth, or Jimmy Carter of Plains, Georgia—I face temptation, too. I fail and I am forgiven as they have been. I am discovering what they discovered. God's answers work! His Word and His people have much to teach us about how they work. Though we may bear scars from our losses, He offers us victory and joy and wonderful surprises all along the way.

Story 1

ADAM AND EVE
(What Was It Like Before Sexual Lust?)

In the very beginning, God had a wonderful sexual fantasy. As Genesis pictures it: "So God created man in his own image . . . male and female created he them . . . . and they shall be one flesh" (Genesis 1:27; 2:24 KJV). Sex has been a part of God's dream for us from the beginning. He didn't snicker or giggle or gasp and turn away when Adam and Eve presented themselves naked for His final clearance check. "God saw all that he had made, and it was very good" (*see* 1:31).

Good? This is the understatement of the ages. Picture it! On the sixth day of Creation God walks in his newly planted garden home. The first rays of sunshine filter through the shade trees. A meadowlark trills his newfound song from the green and leafy branches overhead. Animals feed and frolic on the damp grass, while God trembles with anticipation of what He will create this day.

"And," Genesis records, "the Lord God formed man of the dust of the ground, and breathed into his nostrils the breath of life . . ." (2:7 KJV). Stop right there! Play that scene again. This time replay it in slow motion. After all, you and I are being created, too. We must not speed past this moment, for in every loving stroke of that soft, damp clay we learn about ourselves and about the God who made us.

Watch closely as man evolves from the earth through the
Master Craftsman's hands. Lovingly He forms those com-
plicated systems which sustain us: the circulatory system—heart, arteries, veins, capillaries, and blood pumped
and flowing through them; the respiratory system—nose,
larynx, trachea, and lungs, bringing air into our bodies and
pumping out the poison; the digestive system—canals that
carry and process human fuel through pancreas, bladder,
kidneys, and intestines; the skeletal-muscular system—206
bones and 650 muscles that move and protect them; and the
nervous system—brain, spinal cord, 43 pairs of nerves,
connecting eyes, nose, ears, lungs, heart, and digestive system and regulating all the other systems.

God has worked on this prototype man all day without a
rest—stringing cables, coupling hoses, and testing filters.
All the required systems are now built in but one. So God
bends over that first human model for one last creative
stroke. Since man is being shaped in the image of life's
Creator, man, too, will be given the power to create life.
See God shaping the reproductive system, first in the male
model—testicles, urethra, a penis (later in the female
model—ovaries, uterus, a vagina).

Then, all parts in place, God bends down over the young
man's lifeless form. God's lips cover man's lips, and all
Creation is silent at that scene. Then God breathes His
Spirit into man, and Adam gasps to life. His eyes blink
open. His arms stretch heavenward. Slowly God helps him
to his feet. Creator embraces His creation, and Adam tilts
back his head and laughs a great, booming, joyful laugh that
echoes through the universe. Animals and birds squeak and
bray and whinny and trumpet their reply. Mankind is born.
The life now set in motion will bring us life (and death—but
that comes later). On with the celebration . . . .

Adam turns and runs laughing through the garden, trying out his new body along the way. His eyes squint against the sun to trace the eagle's distant flight. His arms stretch downward. His hand grasps a round stone. His muscles send it skipping across the water. His voice calls out the names of each animal, names his brain invented. His nose sniffs in wonder the fragrance from a field of flowers. His ears pick up the music from a mockingbird darting overhead. His fingers clutch and pull a fruit from its branch. He bites into the bright yellow flesh. Juice trickles down his chin, and Adam laughs again at his discovery of the sweetness of its taste.

God watches man alive, tasting, touching, hearing, seeing, feeling, and God smiles to Himself: "It is good." But after a while, God notices a change in man. He is not laughing anymore. He sits alone on a nearby hillside. His shoulders sag. His eyes stare longingly into space. Something is missing in Creation. Man is lonely. God decides: "It is not good for man to be alone." Man lies back naked in the grass and sleeps, warmed by the sun. Then God goes to work on His second masterpiece of that last day of Creation.

When man awakens he is not alone. A woman, Eve, mother of mankind, sits smiling down at him. Adam stares at her body, so like—and yet so unlike—his own. Her skin is soft. Her body is smooth. Her breasts are round. He reaches out to caress her cheek and trembles at the touch. Something is happening inside them both. Emotion-triggered nerves send messages to the brain. Glands and muscles respond. He takes her in his arms and slowly lowers her to the earth.

It is God's turn now to laugh with joy at what happens next. He has equipped their bodies for this ultimate pleasure. He nods and smiles when they embrace and lie together in the grass. All the splendor that follows were His ideas first. Creation must have given God great pleasure—for look at the pleasure He is giving them in this, *their* first loving act of creation.

The obvious question follows: How did God's dream for His Creation turn into the nightmare that you and I know? It is pictured in this way: In the center of Paradise is the knowledge-of-good-and-evil tree. One morning, as God leads Adam and Eve through their garden home, He pauses before that tree and whispers, "The day you eat of this tree you will surely die." For three thousand years, readers of Genesis have wondered what on earth that tree was all about.

Is God playing some kind of cruel game with man, baiting a trap and waiting for it to spring? No. God loves his created beings and is never cruel. Is God holding back some fruit to keep them hungry and dependent? No. The garden is loaded with fruit trees. In the huge orchard only one is marked OFF LIMITS. Is God trying to keep them ignorant so they will serve Him as His slaves? No. These are intelligent beings whom God has personally designed to supervise His universe and be His friends. God doesn't need ignorant friends any more than we do.

Then what is the mystery in the tree? The answer is simple. God has spoken: "Do not eat from that tree." It is His warning word to them. *Do not eat* means "Obey Me!" Their problem is not to decide for themselves what is good or bad about the tree, but to decide if they will obey God or not. Will Adam and Eve be satisfied to live within this circle of obedience, or will they disobey, step outside it, and pay the consequences?

One bright morning after the warning, Adam swims in the

crystal-clear waters of a lake near the center of Paradise. Eve sits watching him under that tree. She squints sleepily against the sun reflecting off the water. A voice interrupts her reveries and asks, "Is it true that God has forbidden you to eat from any tree in the garden?"

"We may eat the fruit of every tree," she answers, "except the tree in the middle of the garden. God has forbidden us either to eat or to touch the fruit of that one. If we do, we shall die."

The voice answers, "Eve, of course you will not die. God knows that, as soon as you eat it, your eyes will be opened and you will be like God—knowing both good and evil."

Eve turns from watching her husband swim and begins to toy with the forbidden fruit. Touching, smelling, or tasting the fruit is not the issue. Eve is contemplating disobedience. She has lived happily with her husband in God's circle of obedience. He has provided all their needs, asking only that they trust Him enough to obey. Soon both of them will disobey. Together they will step outside the circle of obedience to test God's word for themselves. Why believe Him? Why trust His word when you can find out the hard way that His word was to be trusted all the time?

Adam sees her silhouetted against the sun. What is she holding in her hand? He swims rapidly toward the shore and soon stands beside her. The water still runs in silken rivulets down his naked body. The sun is setting red and golden over Paradise for the last time. It is "sixty seconds and counting" before God's dream for them and us will end.

The voices of generations yet unborn cry out, "Do not disobey!" The victims of Guernica and Dachau and Hiroshima scream the warning. But no one flirting with disobedience thinks about where the act will finally end or who will suffer. We all know that from personal experience. Why blame them? We know how the urge to break free and "do our own thing" can conquer all. Soon Adam and Eve will learn that people are free *only* when they obey God. Disobedience brings slavery. But there on the hillside of Paradise, beneath the knowledge-of-good-and-evil tree, they think that freedom comes through disobeying Him.

So they give in to folly and eat the fruit. *They disobey God.* "Then the eyes of both of them were opened and they discovered that they were naked; so they stitched fig-leaves together and made themselves loincloths" (Genesis 3:7).

What a pathetic picture! They have not become as God, as the evil impulse promised. But their eyes have been opened. They have gained a new perspective on themselves, impossible before that disobedient act. Adam and Eve, the same young lovers who ran naked and free while they remained inside God's circle of obedience, now cringe outside in the bushes, hiding from each other and from Him. Any three-year-old caught with his hand in the cookie jar can explain the new perspective they have gained. They have disobeyed God. Now they have seen themselves not as obedient, trusting children, but as disobedient. This day, for the first time, man and woman feel guilt, and that guilt goes to their core, affecting how they see each other and how they see God.

At this awful moment, God arrives on the scene to walk with them in Paradise at the end of another day.

"Where are you?" God cries.

"We heard you coming," they reply, "and because we were naked we hid."

And the garden echoes wih God's cry of discovery and of grief: "You have disobeyed."

"Yes, Lord, we have disobeyed."

And they know that from that moment of disobedience it will never be the same. Slowly God turns. They follow Him one last time through Paradise. They will not run naked and unashamed before Him again. The days of innocence and uncomplicated joy have ended.

Blinded by their tears and driven outside Paradise by their own disobedience, Adam and Eve stand trembling outside the gate. With one arm, the young man leans against the cold, mossy surface of that high ugly wall. With the other arm he supports his sobbing bride. The sun disappears. The darkness envelops them. It is cold outside and they are alone and afraid.

They both ache with wishing it had never happened. They would give anything to live that moment over again, to obey and turn from the forbidden fruit back to God again. But it is too late. Unable to go back—and afraid to go forward into the future their disobedience has formed for them—Adam sobs quietly the discovery each of us has made: "We do not live in Eden anymore."

Is the story history? Does it really matter if Moses is reporting history as the 6 o'clock news team on Channel 4 defines it, or if he is writing in inspired Hebrew verse a poetic background account for the mess in which man finds himself even today? Who's to say there was no actual garden, no real Adam and Eve? What are we to gain by doubting or debating it? The real question follows: What is God saying to me through this beautiful ancient story, and will I have the good sense to hear and obey Him?

Every generation feels the Eden impulse: to run naked, innocent, unashamed, and unencumbered by guilt. In our own time we have seen them by the thousands: beatniks, flower children, hippies, poor people in desert communes, or rich people on exclusive hideaway beaches and Mediterranean yachts. But their attempts to return to Paradise fail. So will ours.

Even the skeptics agree that there seems to be a garden impulse somewhere in the brain's prehistoric memory bank. Who has not known the longing to return to a place where God and man once walked and talked together in the cool of the day? And though we ache to live in that garden again, disobedience makes it impossible. Like Adam and Eve, we don't live in Eden anymore. Something happened in the garden that conditioned us all. We are no longer innocent.

Still, what happened then to Adam and Eve happens again and again to us. God dreams great dreams for His Creation. Evil lures man away and destroys God's dream. But there is good news! God never stops working to rescue us from our acts of self-destruction.

Note the postscript to that tragic day when Adam and Eve discovered the end of disobedience: "The Lord God made tunics of skins for Adam and his wife and clothed them" (Genesis 3:21). They had chosen to walk away from God, to step outside His circle of obedience, but immediately God set to work to rescue them and bring them home again. Those tunics He draped over their shoulders were to protect them on their journey. It was a sign of His ongoing love for His creatures. They had disobeyed. They would suffer. But God would never stop loving them. God would not abandon them to the cold, in spite of their disobedience. Already He was setting in motion a plan that would rescue His creatures and their heirs, a plan that would end at Easter.

So—what does the story of Adam and Eve have to do with sexual lust? To understand sexual lust we must first understand the wider problem of man's disobedience from the beginning of time and what God is doing to restore His dream in us.

Fifteen years ago, my twelve-year-old brother rode a bicycle down a beautiful park trail in Portland, Oregon. The path wound its way along a scenic reservoir and down through fields of flowers. It was a lovely ride. But near the end of the trail, unknown to my brother, a construction crew had cut through the path to make a road. No warning signs had been posted, no barriers had been built. Suddenly, rounding a corner, the trail ended and dropped forty feet to the road below. My brother hurtled into space and was killed.

Evil works that way. You start down what looks like a beautiful mountain trail. Slowly your speed increases until you lose control and hurtle into space. The beautiful trail is in reality a death trap.

From the first day of man's disobedience, God has carefully marked the trails we ride to death with a one-word sign: SIN! Modern man hates the word, jokes about it, wishes it away. We think that God is the cause of our inconvenience, that He has cut off the good and exciting things. We forget that something is not evil *because* God called it sin. God has called it sin because it *is* evil, destructive to His dream for us, a death trap. God loves us too much to leave those trails unmarked.

Apparently the tree in the garden was a death trap. God so marked it. "Don't eat from this tree or you will die," He warned them. "It will hurt you. It will destroy My dream for you. It will lead to your death."

Read the whole story. See how God kept on warning His disobedient creations. He tried to warn Cain, the son of Adam and Eve, when Cain was jealous of his brother, Abel. God warned: ". . . sin is a demon crouching at the door. It

shall be eager for you, and you will be mastered by it"
(Genesis 4:7). Cain ignored God's warning and murdered
Abel and ended up like his parents, fleeing in shame from
the face of God, "a vagrant and a wanderer on the earth"
(*see* v. 14).

But God kept on warning. To His people, wandering
across the Sinai Desert, God posted his basic list of warnings. They are recorded in the history of the Israelite
exodus from Egypt.

"Do not kill," God warns. "Killing is a sin, a death trap;
it will destroy My dream for you!"—"Do not steal, or lie,
or envy," He warns! "Do not worship any other God or
take My name in vain. Do not commit adultery." The Ten
Commandments and other Old Testament warning signs
along the way are not posted to crimp our style and make us
miserable. These sin signs are posted by a loving Father
who warns that traveling these trails will lead to the destruction of His dream for us and to our death.

Sexual lust is one of the trails that God has marked with
the clear warning sign: DANGER! THIS TRAIL LEADS AWAY
FROM ME. His Word warns us directly or indirectly against
"doing it" or thinking about "doing it":

- With another man's wife or another woman's husband
  (*adultery*)
- With members of your own family (*incest*)
- By force, coercion, trickery, or trap (*rape*)
- Before marriage, during separation, after divorce (*for-
  nication*)
- With one of your own sex (*homosexual lust*)
- With an animal or an object (*awkward lust*)
- By watching others doing it (*peekaboo lust*)
- Just by wishing you were doing it (*lecher lust*)

Add to these the more exotic warnings—including those against sexual intercourse with angels and Moabite women, with temple priests and prostitutes—and it gets pretty obvious. Sexual intercourse practiced apart from heterosexual marriage is forbidden. We may wish it were not so. But God's Word is clear.

It is not that God is against sexual intercourse. Inside God's circle of obedience, sexual intercourse is still God's great gift for pleasure and procreation. A man and a woman, committed to each other in marriage, are free to experience a full range of physical and emotional pleasures from each other's bodies. But outside the circle of obedience, God's gift becomes destructive and dehumanizing. Following that path in spite of His warnings will lead to disaster.

Now, at the beginning, we must decide if we will take these ancient warnings seriously. Apparently, few people in our time think that God really means them. Sexual intercourse outside of marriage seems to be standard procedure even for teen dating. And marriage itself seems more and more a tired old custom best forgotten.

That is why I begin this book about sexual lust "in the beginning." Adam and Eve may seem light-years away from the immediate struggle with sexual lust in your life. The Bible's picture of Paradise, forbidden fruit, and two young lovers who disobey and eat it may appear ridiculously out-of-date and absurdly remote to a sexual affair you are having or are contemplating at this moment. I am sure it *turns you off* to hear my warnings against what *turns you on*, especially when he or she or it seems so appealing, so desirable, and so innocent.

But that was Adam and Eve's big mistake. They looked at the fruit hanging there—so shiny, ripe, and delicious—

and they underestimated what was really going on. That is *our* first mistake as well. We dare not underestimate disobedience. We aren't really making a simple, short-range, innocent, one-night decision any more than they were only eating a piece of fruit. We are deciding, as they were, whether to live inside God's circle of obedience or to step outside that circle, ignore His warnings, and pay the consequences.

When I struggle with my own sexual lust, I think of Adam and Eve and what they lost by stepping outside God's circle of obedience. And it helps me.

SUMMARY

Story 1: Adam and Eve
(What Was It Like Before Sexual Lust?)

In the very beginning, God had a wonderful sexual fantasy. He created a young man and a young woman and placed them in Paradise. He laughed with joy as they ran naked and unashamed through the meadows. He equipped their bodies for pleasure and smiled when they embraced and lay together in the grass. All those ideas were God's ideas first.

Bad news! We don't live in Eden anymore. Don't blame God. Those first young lovers weren't satisfied with God's dream. They ate the fruit, which means they disobeyed God, and their disobedience closed down Paradise. We can never live that innocent, struggle-free life again.

Good news! God never stops working to rescue us from our acts of self-destruction. Carefully He has marked the trails that lead to danger and to death. Sexual lust is one of them. It can destroy God's dream for you.

Genesis 1–3   The Creation Story
Genesis 4:1–15   The Story of Cain and Abel
Exodus 20   The Ten Commandments and Other Warning Signs

Story 2

THE SONS OF GOD AND THE DAUGHTERS OF MEN
(How Did Sexual Lust Get Such a Bad Name?)

The Bible has no lack of explicit sexual details. Human sexuality is a major theme developed throughout the sixty-six books by dozens of authors over a period of thousands of years. From Genesis to Revelation, God's wisdom and warnings about sex come through loud and clear. The Bible is a frank and powerful and practical sex guide.

It isn't all judgment and doom, either. The Bible speaks joyfully and hopefully about sex *inside* God's circle of obedience. Young lovers sing in anticipation of the ecstasy of the marriage bed. Wedding feasts are celebrated. Husbands and wives are given careful instructions as to how to keep their sex life healthy. Sexual hygiene is taught, complete with recommended soaps and perfumes to attract and hold your lover. Humorous ancient proverbs guide lovers past sexual pitfalls. Stories of marriages are told in elaborate detail and act as models for all of us who struggle to keep marriage alive and growing. The Bible furnishes us a library of case studies that illustrate the beauty and joy of sex as God dreams it.

However, the biblical authors tell in equally frank detail what happens when we refuse to heed God's warning about sex outside the circle of obedience. The adult-only, true-life stories in Scripture describe the history of sexual lust on this planet. Settings vary across a wide range of cultures and peoples—from tribesmen wandering in the desert (having intercourse with their sheep) to sophisticates living in great cities where adultery, homosexuality, prostitution, rape, and incest were epidemic.

The first case of sexual lust in Old Testament history occurs only a few dozen lines after the story of Adam and Eve is told. At the beginning of the Bible, in the first book, you can read it:

> And it came to pass, when men began to multiply on the face of the earth, and daughters were born unto them, That the sons of God saw the daughters of men that they were fair; and they took them wives of all which they chose.
>
> Genesis 6:1, 2 KJV

Scholars and lay persons have debated or ignored this story for centuries. Who can blame them? It seems, on the surface, a prehistoric myth more akin to Homer and the lecherous, lusting, leering gods of Mount Olympus than to Moses and the God of Israel.

It is difficult for us to picture a superhuman race equipped physically and emotionally as we are, yet who are more than human. For our pictures of these creatures we might fall back on the Renaissance art of Michelangelo. Perhaps you have stared at the Sistine Chapel wall in the Vatican, fascinated by those winged men from Muscle Beach, who were being cast into the lower regions by their angry Creator. Or perhaps you've trembled with fear as the rebellious angels described by John Milton in *Paradise Lost* withered in the lake of fire.

These artistic giants were inspired by Old Testament

writers who envisioned God seated on a heavenly throne surrounded by His courtiers or servants. This angel corps, created by God to do His bidding, appears and disappears throughout the history of Israel.

Remember the two angelic messengers who visited Abraham to warn him of the fall of Sodom? They were human in appearance and very beautiful, yet when sexually attacked by Abraham's neighbors these angelic visitors showed their superhuman powers by blinding the mob and disappearing.

Remember Jacob, Abraham's grandson, who saw a ladder extending to the feet of God and on the ladder a continual line of angelic servants ascending and descending on God's business? Later, in Peniel, Jacob met one of these angelic beings and wrestled with him through the night, refusing to let him go until the angel had blessed him. The angel was human enough that Jacob would dare attack him; yet, in the fight, one touch of the angel's finger and Jacob's thigh went out of joint.

Read the description of the prophet Micaiah: "I saw the Lord sitting upon his throne, and all the host of heaven standing on his right hand and on his left" (2 Chronicles 18:18 KJV). Or Isaiah's words: ". . . I saw also the Lord sitting upon a throne, high and lifted up . . . . Above it stood the seraphims: each one had six wings . . . . And one cried unto another, and said, Holy, holy holy, is the Lord of hosts . . ." (Isaiah 6:1–3 KJV).

Or remember the visits to Mary and Joseph by a superhuman being who appeared with the good news of her appointment to be the mother of Jesus—or the angelic messengers who visited the shepherds with their announcement of joy to the world?

There are those who walk away laughing from these ac-

counts of a race of angelic supermen created by God to
serve Him. Others believe so literally in every description
of them that they spend centuries debating how many of
them could land safely on the head of a pin.

What we should do, especially with this first story of the
angels' disobedience, is to quit arguing about incidentals,
suspend our disbelief, and try to discover what the story
means. For the account of the angels' mutiny and their
desire for the daughters of men is like the story of the garden and its forbidden fruit. There is more going on than
meets the eye. This first report of sexual lust by angelic
beings becomes a textbook case, illustrating the effect of
sexual lust in the exclusively human cases that follow.

What is going on beneath the surface of this angelic-
human love affair? What could possibly be wrong with boys
from such good stock falling in love with our fair ladies?
Clearly, they had sexual intercourse on the first date, but
according to the Old Testament reports they eventually
married the girls. These are no irresponsible, one-night-
stand types. There is nothing kinky going on here. Besides,
from the account of their marriages, a race of heroes or
giants was born.

Yet the most tragic verse in the Bible appears immediately at the close of the first lust story:

> And God saw that the wickedness of man was great
> in the earth, and that every imagination of the thoughts
> of his heart was only evil continually. And it repented
> the Lord that he had made man on the earth, and it
> grieved him at his heart.
>
> Genesis 6:5, 6 KJV

So God, looking down at this apparently innocent merging
between the sons of God and the daughters of men, is so

angered by its result that He says, "I will destroy man whom I have created from the face of the earth, for I am sad that I have made them" (*see* v. 7).

The story of Noah and the flood follows, a grim reminder of what happened next to mankind. But what happened to the offending angels? Peter continues where the Old Testament writer leaves off: "God did not spare the angels who sinned, but consigned them to the dark pits of hell, where they are reserved for judgement" (2 Peter 2:4). Jude, writer of the shortest New Testament book, refers to this tragedy and compares the lustful angels to the people of Sodom and Gomorrah: ". . . like the angels, they committed fornication and followed unnatural lusts; and they paid the penalty in eternal fire, an example for all to see" (v. 7).

Wait a minute! Doesn't it seem terribly unreasonable for God to drown the human offenders and sentence the guilty angels to hell just because they slept together? Are the rumors true: "God hates sex and really gets mad when he sees anyone enjoying it"? No. Behind this first biblical example of sexual lust is a far greater problem. The angels' sexual lust is only a symptom of something much more deadly going wrong. Their lust for the fair ladies of earth is only the stage on which the greater tragedy is being played, a symptom of their greater disobedience.

Sexual Lust Led to the Destruction of God's Plan for Them

The Apostle Jude explains the real problem this way in verse 6: "Remember too the angels, how some of them were not content to keep the dominion given to them but abandoned their proper home . . . ." To say it more simply, these particular angels were not satisfied with God's plan for them. He had created them to do His bidding. They refused and walked away.

See that awful moment through God's eyes, as He stood watching them sneak away for a night on Planet Earth. Over the past few weeks he had noticed them spying on the daughters of men, winking and whistling after them. Those girls were beautiful. Who can blame the normal, red-blooded angels for being somewhat distracted by the soft, round breasts and smooth, slender thighs swishing by below them! "Boys will be boys," even if they are angels. Right? Why should God get so steamed up about it? Because God knew where it all would end.

God must have warned them early in its stages: "This trail leads away from Me. Follow it and you will die." But they didn't listen. They never dreamed that they would not come back to Him. They liked their jobs. They worshiped their boss. It was no journey away from God, just a rest stop along the way, a temporary diversion, a quick roll in the hay: a lonely lady and a lovely lad—who met by chance—share each other's bodies, then say *good-bye* and it's over.

If we can project onto these angels what we know about the human side from our own struggles with lust, we can guess it began in innocence: a quick glance, a longer stare, rising fantasies, and a night on the town. Then it progressed to repeated trips earthward and weekends away, moving out and settling in. The end of the cycle of sexual lust is predictable. The disobedient angels moved out of their home with God and never came back.

And this moving out is the real tragedy. God is not angry simply because an angelic being made love to a beautiful woman. The issue is not simply sexual lust. What grieved the heart of God was the power of sexual lust to draw the angels away from His domain for them. Sexual lust was the cause of the greater disobedience; the angels forgot who they were and why they had been created.

These deserting angels are the sons of God. He had created them to be His co-workers in His care for the world. They would be His mighty hand, striking down evil and bringing justice to the earth. They would be His arm to free His people, Israel, and guide them through the wilderness. They would be His voice, whispering truth into the prophets' ears and echoing loudly in the brains of His disobedient kings. They would be His feet, running to announce to the shepherds, "Good tidings of great joy; a Saviour is born."

How must God have felt as He watched them leave that day? He heard their boyish laughter and saw their faces flush red with sexual excitement. He had created each of them with a purpose. He loved each one of them as He loved Adam and Eve. They were His children. They had been lovingly and caringly designed to fulfill His dream for them. They had been made to know God and to enjoy Him forever. And suddenly, one view of soft breasts and slim ankles and they are gone.

Sexual Lust Led to the Misuse of God's Power in Them

From the beginning, He had cared for them. If we can project from our experience what must have been theirs, no joy had been withheld. No good thing had been denied. God had gone so far as to share with them His power, giving them rule, dominion, and charge over portions of His Kingdom, as Adam and Eve had been given charge of Paradise. Then He watched them walk away from His dream. He saw them step outside His circle of obedience in which they had lived happily. He stared in disbelief as they wasted their creative power (power given them to do His work in the world) on wooing and winning the women of earth.

And from this marriage of the sons of God and the daughters of men came a race of giants. The details are

sketchy. Apparently, these oversized offspring of the
angels' lust seemed heroic by man's standards but were
distortions in the eyes of God. Through His children's disobedience, God's dream for man and angels became a
nightmare. They lost sight of the difference between good
and evil, and their hearts were given over to evil continually. Away from Him, the power which God had shared
with them became a means of ugliness and death.

Sexual lust led the angels to walk away from God and
misuse their God-given powers. God knew this cycle of
disobedience had to be broken in order that His dream for
His children could begin afresh, as it had in the beginning.
So the tears of God became a flood that drowned all His
Creation save Noah, and through Noah the world was born
again.

You say, "I don't believe in angels." The details of the
story may seem mythical at best. You want more historic
examples to make the point. That's easy. The Bible goes on
to tell in all-too-human terms the same tragic story. The
cycle of sexual lust repeats itself over the centuries. Every
time, it begins in sexual attraction and ends with God's
children's forgetting who they are and why they were
created. Sexual lust begins in the head and quickly moves
on to a one-night stand. It ends with God's children giving
up His dream for them, moving out of the circle of obedience, and into the cycle of disobedience and death.

God warns against sexual lust, not because He hates His
children to enjoy each other's bodies, but because He
knows where disobedience will end. For example, read on
in the history of Israel in Numbers 25: God had just freed
His people from slavery in Egypt. He was leading them
across the wilderness to their new home in the Promised
Land. This forty-year journey was an integral part of God's

plan to rescue the world from the cycle of sin and death. The people on that march had been created for this historic moment. But out there in the heat of the desert it was hard to remember how serious the journey was in the plan of God.

Picture that moment when God's people stumbled into an oasis where the people of Moab lived. Boys who had been born on the march, who had grown to young manhood in the wilderness, and who had never known the comforts of home and hearth were suddenly surrounded by a city with cool, rock-walled buildings, flowing fountains, and clean, sweet-smelling girls—wearing silken dresses, reclining on pillows, and inviting the strangers to share their hospitality.

What could be wrong with one night of pleasure after a lifetime of blistered feet and dirty bodies and parched throats? "Tomorrow we will get back to God's journey. Tonight, we will lie in the arms of the Moabite women."

Sexual Lust Blinded Them to God's Presence With Them

And again God's warning echoed in their ears: "Do not give in to sexual lust." The warning seemed so unreasonable. It was the young men's one chance to experience what they might never be able to experience again. After all, they might die out there in the desert, never having known a woman. They had no intention of making it a permanent relationship. It was a sexual sin, but it could be forgiven in the morning.

So they stepped outside God's circle of obedience. And at sunrise, after their night of ecstasy, the young women of Moab invited them to a special breakfast. Sleepily the young men agreed. Around the heavily laden buffet, God's children watched the curious custom of the Moabite priests' sacrificing to the stone god Baal.

Nights passed. The sun rose and set. One by one the young men joined in the breakfast sacrifice. At first it was just being polite, a trade, giving the girls what they wanted in the morning for giving the boys what they wanted at night. Soon, the Old Testament writer reports: "Israel joined himself to Baal and the anger of the Lord was kindled against His people."

Moses walked from the camp of Israel into the cities of Moab and found the young men living with the Moabite women, worshiping the Moabite god. His pleas to them went unheard. The young men had forgotten who they were and why they had been created. They moved out of the circle of obedience. Without even consciously deciding, they ended their journey with God, moved away from His people, and set up housekeeping with God's enemy.

> And the Lord said unto Moses, Take all the heads of [these young men] and hang them up before the Lord against the sun . . . . And Moses said unto the judges of Israel, Slay ye every one his men that were joined to Baal-peor.
>
> Numbers 25:4, 5 KJV

Twenty-four thousand young men died before the journey could begin again.

We read this ancient story and shudder with horror. We forget that God was waging a war with evil. We forget how seriously He pursues His purpose in the world. We forget how many times He had warned them and how generously He had met their every need along the journey. We forget how much He loved them. These young men were God's children. He had created them to work at His side to rescue the world from evil. Now, in spite of every loving gift He had given them, they deserted His ranks and joined the enemy.

It began in "innocent" sexual lust. It ended with their forgetting who they were and why they had been created. By moving outside God's circle of obedience, they precipitated their own destruction. God had no choice but to signal His faithful children forward and leave the bones of the unfaithful to bleach white in the desert. Two thousand years later the Apostle Paul, pleading with a Corinthian Christian struggling with sexual lust, reminded him of this story and explained, "These things were done to be our example, that we not lust after evil things as they lusted" (*see* 1 Corinthians 10:6).

The story is repeated in the time of the judges after God's people arrived in Israel. Samson had governed them for twenty successful years. God had worked great miracles through Samson's life. Then one day he saw a beautiful young prostitute in Gaza. Why did he go into Delilah's house, strip off his clothes, and lie back on her silken sheets? Although he may have been Israel's equivalent of a senator, a Supreme Court judge, or a President, he was human and struggled with temptation like the rest of us.

Again, it began as a quick one for the road. He would get his relief, pay her handsomely, swear her to secrecy, and be on his way. But every time he passed her apartment on official state business, the bells rang and the horns blew and Samson gave in again. What began as a simple case of sexual lust ended with Samson far from God—his God-given powers wasted, enslaved and blinded by his enemy, humiliated before his people, and finally dead in the collapse of the building which Samson himself pulled down.

The story is repeated in the time of the kings. When he

was old, Solomon the Wise (who built God's house in
Jerusalem) loved women in his harem who served false
gods. He loved to be pampered and caressed by these
young foreign women in his harem. But they made him pay
for his sexual lust. They insisted that Solomon build shrines
to the pagan gods Chemosh and Molech as these women
demanded. The Old Testament writer reports sadly the end
of the old king's lust: "Solomon's heart was turned away
from God and God said, 'I will take thy kingdom from
thee' " (*see* 1 Kings 11:9–11).

By the time of the prophets Jeremiah and Ezekiel, sexual
lust and serving false gods became synonymous. The men
of Israel chased after pagan women and pagan gods with
equal zeal. And Jeremiah cried out the words of the Lord,
"Turn, O backsliding children, saith the Lord; for I am
married unto you . . ." (Jeremiah 3:14 KJV).

The New Testament picks up this theme. We are the
bride of Christ. We are to know Him and be known by Him.
Sexual lust—knowing another man or woman sexually,
outside God's circle of obedience—can destroy God's plan
for us, can misuse God's power in us, and can blind us to
God's presence with us. No wonder sexual lust got its bad
name! It is more than bodies rubbing together for pleasure.
Sexual lust leads us to forget who we are and why we were
created. It can be the beginning of the end of our relationship with Him.

When I struggle with my temptation, I remember the disobedient angels, the wandering sons of Israel, and Samson
and Solomon. I, too, when sexually aroused, may find that I
also enjoy the fantasy that may all too naturally follow, but
I also remember that I am a child of God and that He has
great plans for me. I remember that my powers were given

to me for His purpose. And I remember how quickly sexual lust can lead me away from God, to the place where I quit worshiping Him and walk away from God forever. Those ancient memories help me to control my natural arousal and the fantasies that follow—before they begin the destructive process of lust in me.

SUMMARY

Story 2: The Sons of God and the Daughters of Men
(How Did Sexual Lust Get Such a Bad Name?)

The Bible speaks joyfully and hopefully about sex inside God's circle of obedience. It also tells in frank detail the stories of heartbreak and horror of those who ignored God's warnings against sexual lust and disobeyed Him. The X-rated, true-life tales of the sins of the sons of God, the sons of Israel, and Samson and Solomon illustrate the end result of sexual lust:

1. Sexual lust led to the destruction of God's plan for them.
2. Sexual lust led to the misuse of God's power in them.
3. Sexual lust blinded them to God's presence with them and led them away from Him forever.

Genesis 6:1–7	The Story of the Sons of God and the Daughters of Men
Numbers 25	The Story of the Children of Israel
Judges 13–16	The Story of Samson
1 Kings 11:1–11	The Story of Solomon

Story 3

DAVID AND BATHSHEBA
(How Does God View Sexual Lust?—
A Lesson in Judgment)

Create in me a clean heart, O God,
and put a new and right spirit within me.
Cast me not away from thy presence,
and take not thy holy Spirit from me.
Restore to me the joy of thy salvation,
and uphold me with a willing spirit.
Then I will teach transgressors thy ways,
and sinners will return to thee.

Psalms 51:10–13 RSV

This was a song sung by King David, after the prophet Nathan's shattering pronouncement: "Thou art the man."

No story of sexual lust is more tragic or instructive than the story of David, second king of Israel. That first night, his palace in Jerusalem was mercilessly hot. The humid evening air was sticky-wet and King David lay naked and drenched in sweat on his royal bed. Soon he would join General Joab at the siege of the enemy city of Rabbah. Battle plans, supply routes, maintenance of the kingdom, thieves, pesky flies, and the heat all conspired to give the king a sleepless night.

Finally he rose from his bed and walked still naked to his

private porch overlooking the sleeping city. His eyes squinted against the darkness. Moonlight bathed the city in an eerie yellow light. Torches flickered at the military guardhouse and along the alabaster palace walls. Footsteps of a patrol on duty echoed somewhere down below. Then silence fell again.

David leaned against the cool marble wall and thought gratefully about the past. Thinking about his amazing rise from shepherd boy to king still left him dazzled. The old prophet Samuel had visited David's surprised father, Jesse, looking for God's successor to the throne of Saul. David smiled to himself as he recalled his father's chagrin when all the older brothers were passed over and David, so recently in the field that he still smelled of sheep, was brought into the prophet and anointed future king of Israel.

David reached for the harp that lay near his feet on the palace porch. He tuned and played it idly in the darkness. He recalled that night, soon after his anointing, when—still a shepherd boy—he had met King Saul. "How mighty are the works of God," thought David to himself. "I came that night as minstrel and stayed to be the king." David laughed and plucked on the harp a rolling chord.

God had worked His Master Plan in the life of David, and that restless night he marveled at the glory of it. God had been his strong hand in the fields to help him kill the wild animals that stalked his flock. God had delivered him from Goliath with a divinely guided missile. With God's help he had set the Philistines to flight. God had rescued him from the jealous wrath of Saul. God had blessed him with an army of allies: the prophets Samuel and Nathan, David's many faithful wives, General Joab, and Saul's own son, Jonathan. Rightful successor to the throne, Jonathan had been David's loyal, loving friend from the beginning. On the porch, David sang his praise to the Lord God Yahweh who had been strong and mighty to deliver him.

I will praise thee, O Lord, with my whole heart; I will shew forth all thy marvellous works. I will be glad and rejoice in thee: I will sing praise to thy name, O thou most High.

Psalms 9:1, 2 KJV

David lowered the harp to the ground and leaned against the cool rock wall. A movement on a rooftop just below the palace caught David's eye. His thoughts of praise were interrupted by a scene of indescribable beauty. A woman bathed naked in the moonlight. Apparently, she, too, had found it impossible to sleep and now, innocent and unsuspecting, she poured water over her breasts and thighs. David watched it run in rivulets down her flesh and desired to hold that warm, wet body in his arms.

Quickly David wrapped a light cloak around his shoulders and summoned the guard. In seconds the foot patrol was at his side.

"Who is that woman?" he asked, pointing to the rooftop below.

"Is that not Bathsheba," one of the guards answered, "the daughter of Eliam, and the wife of Uriah the Hittite?"

"Bring her to me," he commanded and dismissed them from his presence.

David leaned across the wall and watched the woman continue her bath. Suddenly a servant interrupted her. They conversed in quiet whispers. The servingwoman pointed at the palace. Bathsheba dried and dressed quickly. David strained to hear her words, to measure any sign of anger or emotion. The woman draped in fine linens turned and stared for a moment at the shadow of David's mighty palace, then hurried in to prepare to meet the king.

David bathed and lay back on his bed, waiting for the servants to announce Bathsheba's presence. The Old Testament reports in flat, emotionless terms the king's sexual lust: ". . . she came in unto him, and he lay with her; for she was purified from her uncleanness: and she returned unto her house" (2 Samuel 11:4 KJV).

A king can have anything he wants if he is willing to pay the price. But David had no idea how high that price would be. The writer of Second Samuel reports that Bathsheba conceived a child and sent a messenger to tell King David that she was pregnant. Already David's sexual lust had caused the king of Israel to break three of the Ten Commandments. He had coveted his neighbor's wife. He had stolen her from her husband, Uriah the Hittite. And he had committed adultery with her. Now she was pregnant, and David would have to break two more Commandments to cover his tracks. That same day he sent a runner to the front lines with a message to General Joab saying, "Send me Uriah."

It is obvious what David hoped to do. If he could get Uriah home from the battlefield on the pretense of delivering an important message, Uriah would then spend a night with his wife, Bathsheba, and the child, already growing in her, would then be thought to be his child and not the king's.

Uriah finally arrived from the siege of Rabbah. David greeted him with a fond embrace and asked him for a complete report as to how the battle raged. At the close of this masquerade, David instructed his loyal soldier to return home and rest. The king even sent steaks and wine for the welcome-home barbecue that he hoped Bathsheba would prepare for her weary husband's arrival.

David slept easily that night for the first time in days. At

breakfast he mentioned casually to an aide how fortunate
for Uriah to have even one night with such a beautiful wife.

"But, Your Majesty," answered the aide, "Uriah slept
all night outside your door with his servants, where he now
awaits you."

"What?" shouted the king. "Why? Send him to me."
Immediately Uriah was ushered into the king's cham-
bers. David, his emotions held in check, asked discreetly,
"Why, Uriah, after such a long journey, did you not go
home and sleep on your own bed with your waiting wife?"
The prophet reports Uriah's incredible reply:

. . . The ark, and Israel, and Judah, abide in tents;
and my lord Joab, and the servants of my lord, are
encamped in the open fields; shall I then go into mine
house, to eat and to drink, and to lie with my wife? as
thou livest, and as thy soul liveth, I will not do this
thing.

2 Samuel 11:11 KJV

How could David avoid being chastened by the beauty
and the boldness of this reply? He must have felt the ugliness of his sexual lust, in the light of this man's love and
loyalty. What a moment for the king to confess openly his
sin, to beg Uriah's forgiveness—and for the king to return
with his comrade to the field of battle where he belonged.

Instead, David made the poor man stay another night.
And that night at dinner he forced Uriah to drink too much
wine. Obviously, the king hoped that Uriah's drunkenness
would overcome his loyalty and honor and lead him to
Bathsheba's bed. But King David watched Uriah stagger
from the royal banquet hall into the camp of his servants
and sprawl there to sleep on the hard, damp earth.

Did David stand over the sleeping soldier that night, feel
the deepening dilemma and wonder what to do next?

Perhaps it was then the evil plan was born in him. In the morning David wrote a letter to General Joab and sent the letter with Uriah back to the war zone. Joab read the letter from his commander-in-chief and obeyed its ugly request. Uriah was sent by David's command to the front lines where the hottest battle raged. Secretly his comrades were then ordered back, abandoning Uriah to be struck down by the enemy and to die on the field of battle.

In hours the terrible deed was done. The body of the brave and loyal Uriah lay twisted and grotesque in the no-man's-land between the enemy lines. David had finally covered his sin of sexual lust with the sins of deception and murder.

David heard the news of his loyal officer's death. He mumbled something to the messenger about how the "sword devoureth one as well as another," shrugged off his loss, and sent orders for Joab to win the battle. Why did the king not rush from that noisy assembly hall to the stillness of his private chambers? Why did he not fall on his face there before God in confession and grief for the sins on his hands? The Bible doesn't say, but you and I know how the incredible power of sexual lust could blind even David to all but one fact: He wanted Bathsheba and he was willing to lose everything to gain her.

The Bible reports that when Bathsheba's period of mourning had ended, David sent for Bathsheba and she became his wife and bore him a son. But there would be no time for smiling royal pictures. There would be no quick and happy ending to this love affair. In the last sentence of the last verse of chapter 11, which tells this tale of sexual lust, the prophet writes these words: "But the thing that David had done displeased the Lord."

Suddenly into the story comes a reminder of God's righteous presence on the scene. He had been there all the time. Neither secret plan nor whispered order had gone unnoticed by David's Lord. Neither sexual fantasy nor lustful sexual act escaped God's eyes. Now King David must pay for his sin.

Before we judge God too harshly for what He was about to do to bring David's evil acts to justice, remember that David had been warned. He was the king. He knew since childhood the difference between right and wrong. He had been God's servant to protect and promote the law in all the land. There was no question about David's guilt. He knew what was right and what was wrong in God's sight. He heard God's warnings. But he ignored them.

Remember, too, that David had not exactly suffered for honoring and keeping the Law of God in the past. This is David the Psalmist who immortalized his gratitude for all those wonderful, unmerited gifts which God had given him. "How excellent is thy loving-kindness, O God!" David wrote. "The earth is full of the goodness of the Lord," sang David. "The statutes of the Lord are right," confessed David, "rejoicing the heart." (*See* Psalms 36:7; 33:5; 19:8.)

David had seen in his own life the joy that comes in keeping God's commands. He had experienced the flow of blessing that comes from obeying God's righteous word. So everything that God was about to do in judgment on David's disobedience can only be seen as proper and necessary. For God's love must have two sides. Without justice, there can be no mercy. In a world where "love is never having to say, 'I'm sorry,' " there is in the end no love at all.

For a time in David's court, things went on as normal. I wonder if David thought during that lull before the storm, *I got away with it.* Or was he torn by guilt and remorse? The

Bible doesn't say. David went on performing his duties: collecting taxes, making laws, judging the people, sentencing criminals, waging war, planning the temple, leading the people in worship and in sacrifice to God. All seemed normal until the day a runner reported that the prophet Nathan had left his home in the wilderness and that the old man, staff in hand, was marching towards the city.

All the Bible reports about this moment is: "And the Lord sent Nathan unto David . . ." (2 Samuel 12:1 KJV). Perhaps the prophet surprised the entire court that day and walked in to meet the king unannounced. Did Nathan interrupt David's polite greetings and his offering of food and drink? Did the king stand awkwardly before the prophet as the old man told his parable? Was the room filled with military advisors and regional governors, David's close friends and family—all frozen in place and fascinated by the prophet's tale? The story went like this:

> Once there were two men in one city: the one rich, the other poor. The rich man had many flocks and herds; but the poor man had nothing save one little lamb which he had bought and cared for. And the lamb grew up with the poor man and his children as one of the family, a pet who ate and drank and slept with them as though a son or daughter.
>
> One day there came a traveler unto the rich man. But the rich man was unwilling to slaughter one of his many sheep for his guest to eat and instead took the poor man's pet lamb, killed it, and prepared it for the feast.
>
> *See* 2 Samuel 12:1–4

David turned and walked to his throne, symbol of his kingly right to judge the people. In that chair he had heard a thousand stories of criminal acts and had made a thousand judgments on behalf of justice in the land. This story made David angry, so he shouted to his court to make an example of this wicked fellow: "... As the Lord liveth, the man that hath done this thing shall surely die" (v. 5 KJV).

For a moment silence hung above the court. All eyes were fixed on the prophet. Then Nathan said to David, "Thou art the man!" How did David maintain any modicum of poise? How did he keep from running from the room as the prophet went on to tell all?

Thus says the Lord God of Israel, "I anointed you king over Israel and I delivered you out of the hand of Saul, and I gave you the king's house and the king's wives and the king's lands, Israel and Judah. And [said God through Nathan, His prophet] if that had been too little I would gladly have given you more. Therefore, in light of all this, why have you despised My commandment? Why have you done this evil . . . ?"

See 2 Samuel 12:7-9

The court gasped and whispered in disbelief as Nathan named the charges against the king: "You have killed Uriah and you have taken his wife to be your own."

Then, after the charges had gone undenied, Nathan proceeded to announce the penalty for David's sin: "First," said the prophet, "the sword shall never depart from your house; and second, evil will raise up against you from your own family."

Slowly David stood and walked down from the royal throne of judgment to stand his turn in the place of the condemned. The king stood before the messenger of God. His face was drained of color. His body shook. His voice trembled. Finally he fell on his knees before the prophet and confessed, "Nathan, I have sinned against the Lord."

Nathan answered quietly, "And the Lord has forgiven

your sin. You will not die, but because your evil deed has given God's enemies this great chance to ridicule and deny Him, the child that will be born unto thee shall surely die."

That hot, restless night when David took Bathsheba in his arms was long since forgotten. The pleasure that came from that passing moment of sexual lust soon gave way to permanent pain. And it all happened so quickly. In one passing instant, his rooftop fantasy became his trial for murder. Could it be that from one act of sexual lust everyone, including God, is made to suffer?

Immediately the sentence was carried out on his infant son. David tore his royal clothing as a sign of grief and sorrow. He refused to eat and lay on the cold damp ground for seven days and nights. He cried out to God to save his child. But on the seventh day the child died.

When the news reached David, he returned to his quarters, dressed, and went in to worship the Lord. Though God's judgment is sure, the very next verse in chapter 12 gives us proof of God's continuing mercy: "And David comforted Bathsheba his wife, and went in unto her, and lay with her: and she bare [another] son, and he called his name Solomon: and the Lord loved him" (v. 24 KJV).

Centuries later, the Apostle Paul summarized God's overview of David's life with these words: "I have selected David, son of Jesse, a man after my own heart who will do all my will" (*see* Acts 13:22). God's forgiveness of David, and His continued blessing of the king and his descendants, should help all of us who have failed to remember that God can forgive and use us again.

David continued paying for his crimes throughout his lifetime. His sins set in motion a natural process that fulfilled the prophet's prediction that the sword would never leave his house at peace (and that evil would rise up against him from his own family).

In 2 Samuel 13 we learn of David's firstborn son, Amnon, who fell madly in love with his own half sister, Tamar. He and his cunning friend, Jonadab, lay a trap for lovely Tamar. Amnon pretended to be ill and urged David to send Tamar to nurse him back to health again. So she obeyed her father and brought food to her half brother.

When she brought the cakes and wine, Amnon took hold of her arm and began to beg her to get in bed beside him. The Bible reports that the girl refused, saying, "No such thing should be done in Israel." But again sexual lust prevailed in David's family, and Amnon, being stronger than his sister, forced her onto his bed and raped her. Amnon, like his father, got what he wanted and soon after had to pay the price in his own blood.

Absalom, David's third son, was born of Maacah, Tamar's mother, daughter of a neighboring king. Absalom hated Amnon, his half brother, for shaming his sister. But he hid his hatred and catered a banquet for Amnon instead. At the height of Amnon's merrymaking, when the young man was full of wine, Absalom and his accomplices suddenly turned on Amnon and killed David's firstborn son with their swords.

The king continued his self-caused suffering. David tore his clothing and lay on the dirt, crying out for his murdered son and for his shamed Tamar and for the guilt and grief he felt towards both of them.

Years passed. The next few chapters of Second Samuel continue the tragic tale. Absalom received his father's forgiveness, for the king loved this son deeply. But Absalom was not content to be a prince. He wanted the kingdom and so conspired to win the throne of David for himself. During the civil war that followed, David must have remembered the promise of the prophet Nathan, that evil would rise up against him from his own house and that the sword would plague him forever. Seeing his own guilt in his son's conspiracy, David ordered his army to save Absalom's life at all costs.

During a crucial battle, Absalom rode his mule beneath a great brush oak and his long hair was caught in the tangled branches of the tree. For a moment he hung helplessly. General Joab, closer than a brother to his king, rushed to the scene, ignored David's warnings and stabbed Absalom through the heart with three daggers. The soldiers tossed the corpse of David's rebellious son into a great open pit and laid a heap of heavy stones upon him.

There is no more tragic a moment in all of history than the scene that followed. David's troops had won the battle. The rebellion had been put down. And David, surrounded by his cheering soldiers, asked again and again, "What news do you have of my son? Is the young man Absalom safe?"

The room grew strangely quiet. Generals and privates turned away. The secret of Absalom's death was no easy burden to bear. Finally a messenger arrived from the battlefield. The king sobbed out his question once again. "Is my son alive?" And the soldier answered, "All your enemies are dead, my Lord King."

And David screamed out his grief: "O my son Absalom, my son, my son Absalom! would God I had died for thee, O Absalom, my son, my son!" (2 Samuel 18:33 KJV). His guilt and his grief—brought on by one night of sexual lust—lived on in David's life forever.

When I struggle with my own sexual lust, I think of David and the price he paid for a night of passion. But I also remember the price his friends and family paid. How easy it is to forget the suffering our sin will bring to others. Some might blame God or the prophet Nathan, but David himself set the tragic chain of events in motion. It helps me to remember that.

SUMMARY

Story 3: David and Bathsheba—A Lesson in Judgment
(How Does God View Sexual Lust?)

David the Psalmist, king of Israel, had everything a man could desire. Yet, in one night of sexual lust, he set in motion the age-old process that did not stop until it destroyed David's dreams for himself and his family.

1. He was sexually aroused by another man's wife.
2. He desired her (sexual lust as fantasy).
3. He took her (sexual lust as act).
4. He grew afraid of being discovered.
5. He lied and murdered to cover his sexual lust. (One sin leads to another.)
6. He was discovered anyway.
7. He confessed and was forgiven. (His son Solomon is proof of God's grace.)
8. Nevertheless, David was disgraced and dishonored.
9. His family turned against him and against each other.
10. He suffered the long-term consequences of his sexual lust forever.

---

2 Samuel 11–18   The Story of David and Bathsheba
Psalm 51   David's Psalm of New Beginnings

Story 4

HOSEA AND GOMER

(How Does God View the Person Who Lusts?— A Lesson in Grace)

The prophet Hosea was a fiery young preacher whose words of wrath and warning chilled the hot blood of the disobedient people of God. But it wasn't his sermons they remembered most. God chose Hosea to live out a tragic story of sexual lust, as a warning to the Israelites of their lust for pagan gods. In Hosea's story, sexual lust and turning from God are intimately connected. Much of the historic details must be read between the lines, but Hosea's own words of warning and of grace will guide us to the central point which his life and teaching make for those of us who struggle with sexual lust today.

We begin the account when Hosea was in his late teens or early twenties. He was ready for marriage, and his parents encouraged him to find a nice Israelite girl and settle down in the Beeri family bakery. (It might have been a Beeri farm. Hosea's use of illustrations from baking and from farming are the only biographical clues we find in his ancient writings. The rest of the details must come from our imaginations.) Hosea's parents might have dreamed of branch bakeries in Bethel, capital of Israel, and Jerusalem, capital of Judah. For those were the days of Uzziah and Jeroboam, strong kings whose reigns led to prosperity and to peace.

Though the borders between the two feuding states were

often scenes of open hostility and bloody battles, the current joke in Beeri's Bakery was that, since soldiers on both sides had to eat, "Come war or peace, the bread would rise above politics." Hosea's future was secure.

But Hosea was unhappy working with the trays of fresh, hot pastries. He tried to keep his mind on making change and recording sales in the shop. But after a few hours, Hosea would wander down beneath the trees near the river to study the Torah and talk religion with anyone who would listen. His father shook the flour off his apron and shrugged. His hands gestured helplessly. His eyes rolled heavenward, "What can I do? From the beginning he is more interested in Yahweh than in bread. Still, baker or rabbi, one day soon he must be married."

From his childhood, Hosea had been a seeker. He hung around the local shrine, when he should have been at play. He asked questions of the rabbis when he should have been learning his father's trade. Later he used every possible excuse to deliver bakery goods to the capital in order to visit the holy places and watch the sacrifices at the altar of Yahweh. It wasn't as though he were disinterested in marriage. He was, as he had always been, more interested in God. He wanted God's wisdom for this important decision and so he prayed and waited.

Then one day it came to him. The Old Testament writer reports:

> The word of the Lord that came unto Hosea, the son of Beeri, in the days of Uzziah . . . and in the days of Jeroboam the son of Joash, king of Israel . . . . Go, take unto thee a wife of whoredoms . . . for the land hath committed great whoredom, departing from the Lord.
>
> Hosea 1:1, 2 KJV

To put it in the vernacular, God told Hosea to marry a prostitute. And so he did.

The Bible gives no details about where or how they met. But anyone who has seen the beautiful young women of the Near East knows that Hosea could easily have fallen in love with Gomer before God's words confirmed and encouraged their marriage. It would have been easy to hide her profession, at first. Hosea's courtship and marriage might have been as natural and proper on the surface as that of any other Jewish girl and boy in town.

It isn't hard to picture her dark, flashing, Mediterranean eyes. She was a professional. She knew how to drape her lithe, shapely body so that every sensuous curve was displayed with perfection. Was it her pouty cheeks or her sultry eyes that drew him to her? Was it her laughter echoing through the narrow streets or her fond and silent smile that attracted him?

Maybe, as some would tell it, on God's orders he went down into that part of town which good boys never visit and picked the first girl waiting on the first corner and said point-blank, "Marry me." But I can't believe it was that simple. My suspicion is that, although Hosea was a man of God, he was still a man. And by all our evidence he loved that woman as God loved His people, Israel. And he knew her, as God knew the Israelites.

He knew her through his eyes as she walked through their home or prepared the evening meal or played with their three children, two boys and a girl. He knew her through his ears, sharing those long conversations in the evening as they reclined on soft pillows and drank wine and laughed together. He knew her through his body as they shared the most intimate sexual relationships. He knew her through his head as he worked to figure how to pay the bills which she ran up for clothing, spices, and perfumes. And he knew her through his heart, through the pain and the sorrow and the heartbreak her weakness caused him.

For one day Gomer felt the urge to ply her trade again. It is easy to imagine Hosea's dream that in their marriage she would change. If he were at all human, he must have hoped that his great love for her would destroy her need for one-night stands with lovers off the street. He planned that, as she received from his generous hands her food and clothing, a home, and children, she would become a one-man woman, loyal to him alone. How could she not be changed by the kind of love that forgave her past and filled her present with every good thing she dreamed about?

It didn't work. Even after years of marriage, late at night when the music echoed from the inns nearby and the evening air carried the wine-slurred laughter of handsome young men in the street, Gomer would slide silently from Hosea's bed, slip into a silken evening dress and hurry off to rendezvous with any man who wanted her. In spite of Hosea's love, in spite of Hosea's faithfulness, in spite of Hosea's pleas and commands and threats, Gomer shared her body with a line of men who waited at night just outside the prophet's door. In the morning when Hosea found her lying in the streets, through her drunken stupor she didn't even know him anymore.

The sadness and the ugliness of this picture must be read on two levels at the same time. For Hosea it is a personal tragedy brought on by Gomer's sexual lust. For God it was a picture of His people, Israel.

Hosea tells the tale of God's personal tragedy alongside his own. "When Israel was a child, I loved him," God says. "Out of Egypt I delivered my son. But no one in Israel knows me anymore." In the fourteen short chapters of Hosea there are twenty-five passages that deal directly or indirectly with His charge: "The people do not know God."

To the Jews, knowledge is not a stuffy, academic word reserved for dusty libraries and long-winded lectures. In the Old Testament, the root word for "to know" is used over one thousand times. Knowledge of one person by another was intimately gained through observation, conversation, reflection, caring for or paying attention to, and even through sexual intercourse. Remember: "And Adam *knew* Eve his wife; and she conceived, and bare Cain . . ." (Genesis 4:1 KJV). Or later in Genesis, when the men of Sodom desired homosexual relationships with Lot's visitors, they asked, "Where are the men who came to you tonight? Bring them out, that we might *know* them" (*see* Genesis 19:4, 5).

God longed to know His children intimately and be known intimately by them. And He did everything He could to bring about this relationship. He knew them in the beginning when He created them from the earth. He knew them in Egypt when He formed a people and rescued them from the brickworks and rock quarries of Pharaoh. He knew them in their trek through the wilderness with bread from heaven and water from the rocks. He knew them safely across the uncharted deserts with a cloud by day and a pillar of fire by night.

On Mount Sinai God made His covenant with them (not unlike a marriage contract), promising that He would be their God and they would be His people. (He would know them and they would know Him.) The law which God gave to Moses was His gift to instruct the people how to know (or relate to) Him and how to know (or relate to) each other.

True to His promise, God overwhelmed the enemy of His people and led them safely to the Promised Land.

Now, as we look back, as we remember the endless generous, loving gifts which God gave His children, Israel, it seems impossible that time and time again they could forget Him so quickly. No sooner had He acted on their behalf than they disobeyed His laws, ignored His spokesmen, and even worshiped false, man-made gods of stone and clay. So God sent prophets like Hosea to help them to remember Him again. It was a hopeless task, for even when they remembered Him for a while it wasn't long until they forgot again.

Imagine how God must have felt as He watched His own children—for whom He had done so much—living as though they had never even heard His name: disobeying His laws and worshiping idols. Hosea says it well:

> O Ephraim [Israel], how shall I deal with you? How shall I deal with you, Judah? Your loyalty to me is like the morning mist, like dew that vanishes early. Therefore have I lashed you through the prophets and torn you to shreds with my words; loyalty is my desire . . . the knowledge of God.
>
> Hosea 6:4–6

Clear as the prophet's words may be in describing God's feelings, Hosea's own tragedy makes them clearer. Picture him in the early morning, searching for his wife again. Finally, he finds her lying drunk in the gutter after another night with her lovers. Slowly he leans down to help her to her feet. But she jerks away, crying. "I don't know you, old man. Go away!"

Hosea's dilemma with his wife was God's dilemma with His people. That is why I interrupted the story of Gomer's sexual lust to relate it to the larger problem of Israel. Like the prophet's wife, the people had developed lust into a real art form. Hosea cried out against them: "My people . . .

have gone a whoring from under their God" (Hosea 4:12
KJV). Apparently the Jews had forgotten God and knew
only the bankrupt values and man-made gods of their pagan
neighbors. As a result, their relationship to each other had
degenerated into a cycle of lust for each other's bodies,
houses, property, money, and power. To forget God and to
use and mistreat your neighbor is the anatomy of lust.

To Overcome Lust Is to Know God

The solution can be found in Hosea's cry that there is
"no knowledge of God in the land" (*see* 4:1). The crowds
listening to the prophet's loud charge must have laughed
and jeered their reply: "You are crazy, old man. We know
God. Look around you. At Sabbath the synagogues are
crowded. The offering baskets overflow. On feast days our
hymns of praise echo through the land, and the smell of our
burning sacrifices lie pungent on the air."

Hosea continually shouts back at them God's reply: "I
want mercy, not sacrifice." (Quit worshiping Me on Sabbath and using and mistreating your neighbor the rest of the
week.) "I want knowledge of God more than burnt offerings." (I don't want your money. I want to know and be
known by you again.)

Hosea is saying to them (and to us) that sexual lust is only
a symptom of the greater problem: The people don't know
God. They talk, sing, preach, and pray about Him. They
build churches and give offerings in His name, but they
don't really know Him intimately, as He wants to be
known. This is why this story is exciting to all of us who
struggle with sexual lust. Hosea gives us important clues as
to how we can overcome the real problem behind lust in all
its forms, how we can once again know God and His will for
our lives.

How Can We Know God Again?

First, he instructs Israel, if you want to know God, you must obey Him. Perhaps adding to Hosea and Gomer's story can help us understand this first requirement. Picture it! The prophet finds his drunken wife in the streets and carries her home after her whoring. He bathes away the night's filth and sits beside her over cups of spiced tea, waiting for her to sober up again.

Gradually the ugly reality dawns on Gomer. She sees the fresh bruises and runs her fingers through her tangled hair. She vaguely remembers the disgusting state Hosea found her in. Again she has shamed them both. Only this time, imagine that she cries out to Hosea, "I'm sorry, husband. Tell me how I can quit this ugly habit and start our relationship over again."

1. To know God is to obey Him.   Hosea looks at her with compassion, and his thoughts are the thoughts of God answering all of us who ask how we can begin anew. The first clue from the prophet is "Obey!"

To Gomer he may have said it this way: "Tonight, when you hear the music on the evening breeze; when handsome young strangers, cash in hand, line up outside your door; when your heart aches to lie with them again—you must not go. You must obey me."

Remember, we are using Hosea to act out in human terms God's Word for us. To know God is to obey Him. When He says, "Thou shalt not . . ." He means it—and if you really want to know Him, you had better obey Him!

If Gomer felt as I feel when I hear that ominous command to *obey God,* she trembled with fear, or arched her back in defiance: "Obey God? There is so much to obey. I have tried and failed before. I am afraid to try again. I will never be perfect. Why try? It will only lead to more disappointment."

Here Hosea puts his arm around his trembling wife and whispers comfort, as God puts His arms around any of us who are afraid of failing and whispers comfort. Obedience is *one step at a time.* "Don't worry; I will help you. No one asks that you obey perfectly. I will teach you. I will never leave you nor forsake you. And if you fail, I will be there to forgive you and to help you begin again. It will take a lifetime, but together we can do it!"

Tearfully, Gomer agrees to another try. The children are in bed now. Darkness covers the city and the music begins to play. Gomer pretends she doesn't hear it. Tonight she will obey. Tonight she will not go. Then she hears the whispers of the young men outside her door. The old feelings rise in her again. The music plays louder. The young men call out to her. Gomer sinks to the floor. Her hands cover her ears, trying to block out the sound of temptation. She closes her eyes and turns from the window—but she cannot turn off that picture of their arms held out to her. Her teeth are clenched. Her body trembles as she sits crumpled on the floor at her husband's feet. Gomer is determined to last out that night—*obediently.*

2. To know God is to love Him. Hosea watches her struggle, then sits beside her on the floor. Lovingly he takes her hands down from her ears and holds her in his arms. Then he whispers the second step on the road to knowing himself *and God* again: "There is more to *knowing* than obedience. I want you to love me, not just obey me."

Again Gomer reacts for all of us. How can she love this godly old man when young men, strong and sexy, wait just outside the door? How can she love him enough to overcome the lust she has for them? We understand her predicament. Who of us has never asked, "How can I love God—whom I cannot see—enough to overcome the sexual lust I have for those I see all too clearly?"

Look into Hosea's heart, Gomer, as we look into the heart of God. Think about him. Remember how much he loves you. Remember his generous gifts. Remember his dreams for your life. Remember how much more he is worth to you than those young men outside, who trade you a moment of pleasure for a lifetime of pain.

Love takes work, Gomer. Love takes memory and imagination. Even love you fall into must be worked on to last. When the music plays and the young lovers call out your name, think about his love and what losing it will mean to you.

3. *To know God is a lifelong relationship.* What if that next morning Hosea awakened to find fresh flowers on the bedstand and fresh coffee brewing in the kitchen? What if Gomer set about to build their relationship? For that is the third point Hosea makes in instructing Israel how the people can know God again. He calls them to that lifelong process of keeping love alive through a growing relationship. It is Gomer's serving her husband breakfast in bed. It is Hosea's taking the day off to spend it with his wife. It is Gomer's whispering crazy, loving suggestions into her husband's ear, and Hosea's acting on those suggestions. Knowing is a creative, lifelong, needing-to-be-worked-at process in human terms. But we need to be just as creative in maintaining closeness with God.

He wants us to be alone with Him a part of every day, to talk with Him, to share our most intimate secrets with Him. It is hard at first to pray. You may feel silly walking through the hills with your silent, invisible Partner, sharing your intimate feelings with Him. But through the ages those who have tried have discovered the reality of a personal relationship with God, as Hosea promised. They knew God because they continued working at it.

But for most of Israel, as for Gomer, the story has no happy ending. I created this fantasy only to illustrate Hosea's words: To know God (and thus to overcome your lust) you must (1) obey God; (2) love God; and (3) have fellowship with God day by day.

Gomer, like the people of God, refused to try it. It seemed so unrelated to their struggle. It reeked of religious school and sermons and calls to devotion time. It seemed so spiritual, so other-worldly, so unreal in comparison to the reality of those feelings she had when, late at night as she lay on her bed, the music began to play again. As she lay there beside the man of God, she could picture the young men who waited just outside her door. They were more real to Gomer than Hosea because she had no imagination, no memory, no greater commitment.

And so, night after night, Gomer waited until she thought her husband was asleep. Then, like a thief, the silly woman tiptoed silently from the room to another rendezvous with sexual lust. And the prophet lay beside her, wide-awake but helpless. For, like God, he could not force the one he loved to know and love him in return. He lay there scarcely breathing, waiting for her to decide between them. How do you think he felt when she began to move away from him again? He loved her as God loves His children and had to watch her helplessly—as God watched His people forget Him and sneak away.

But this is not where the story really ended. In the morning, when Hosea had their children dressed and off to school, he would head down into that part of town where the cheap bars and twenty-four-hour coffee shops never closed. He would search for her where the massage-parlor lamps flashed their gaudy invitation and the broken-lettered marquees advertised continuous thrills for seventy-five cents a seat. And, in the hangover glow of early morning, he would find her wandering the streets . . . .

For a moment he stares across the piles of garbage, as the woman he loved staggers by without knowing him. She is drunk from drowning out the awful guilt and fear already working in her. Her hair is disheveled. Her clothing is torn and dirty. Her arms are bruised, her shoulders stooped. She staggers and almost falls, but Hosea runs to her side and takes her in his arms again.

"Who are you?" she asks, staring up at him blurry-eyed and bewildered. "I am the one who loves you," he replies. And as the brokenhearted old man takes her in his arms and carries her home again, we hear the Word of God crying out to His children, Israel:

> But I have [loved you] since your days in Egypt, when you knew no other saviour than me . . . . I cared for you in the wilderness, in a land of burning heat, as if you were in pasture. So [you] were filled, and being filled, grew proud; and so [you] forgot me.
>
> Hosea 13:4–6

God is saying, "The more I called, the further you went from Me. The more I called, the more you rebelled."

The picture of the prophet carrying his whoring wife home through the littered streets is one of the Scriptures' most unforgettable illustrations of God's incredible love for us. Hosea will bathe his wife and help her change into clean, fresh clothing. He will fix her something warm to drink and wait beside her until she is sober once again. He will shield her shame from the neighbors and their children.

He will go on loving her, caring for her, knowing her, in spite of all the anger and the disappointment and the shame he feels. And he will do all this, knowing that when the sun sets and the music begins to play again, when the streets echo with the laughter of her lovers, she will steal away from him again.

Was it in such a moment, torn by his own anger and his love toward Gomer that Hosea wrote these ancient words of God:

> How can I give you up, Ephraim, how surrender you, Israel? . . . My heart is changed within me, my remorse kindles already. I will not let loose my fury, I will not turn round and destroy [you]; for I am God and not a man, the Holy one in your midst.
>
> Turn back . . . by God's help, practise loyalty and justice and wait always upon your God.
>
> Return . . . to the Lord your God; for you have stumbled in your evil courses.
>
> I will heal [you] . . . for my anger is turned away . . . .
>
> Hosea 11:8, 9; 12:6; 14:1, 4

The last verse in Hosea's writings is for all of us: "Let the wise consider these things . . . for the Lord's ways are straight and the righteous walk in them, while sinners stumble" (14:9).

When I struggle with my own sexual lust, I remember Hosea carrying Gomer through the streets, and I think about how much God loves me. And it helps.

SUMMARY

Story 4: Hosea and Gomer—A Lesson in Grace
(How Does God View the Person Who Lusts?)

Through the tragic story of the prophet Hosea's love for the prostitute Gomer, we learn that knowing God is a primary solution to spiritual unfaithfulness, and also to the specific problem of sexual lust. Hosea teaches us that to know God requires the following:

1. To know God is to *obey* God.
2. To know God is to *love* God.
3. To know God is to *fellowship* with God forever.

Hosea's unfailing love for Gomer is an unforgettable picture of God's unfailing love for all of us.

Hosea 1–14   The Story of Hosea and Gomer

Story 5

JESUS' TEMPTATION IN THE WILDERNESS

(How Should I Respond to My Own Sexual Lust?)

Jesus was tempted, even as we are. We do not know the details. It is enough to know the fact. The first-century writer of Hebrews reports that "[Jesus] is not a high priest unable to sympathize with our weaknesses, but one who, because of his likeness to us, has been tested every way, only without sin" (Hebrews 4:15, 16). Since He was tempted, and since He survived the temptation without giving in, He is the perfect One to be asked, "How did You overcome temptation?"

To find how Jesus resisted temptation, we return to the wilderness near Jerusalem, where His ministry began. Immediately following His baptism in the River Jordan, Jesus turned and walked away from the crowds into the hot, dangerous desert regions that stretched down from Jericho to the Dead Sea. Anyone who has driven in air-conditioned comfort through these badlands remembers the bare, undulating hills and the dirty-gray sand, wind-whipped into mountainous drifts.

Luke the Physician describes Jesus' journey this way: "Full of the Holy Spirit, Jesus returned from the Jordan, and for forty days was led by the Spirit up and down the

wilderness and tempted by the devil . . ." (4:1, 2). It is a
grim but accurate picture of Jesus' life: a journey through
the wilderness, led by the Spirit and tempted by the devil.

Life Is Wilderness

As we watch Jesus head out into the desert to struggle
with temptation, we are reminded that in at least one way
life is a lot like that for everyone—a journey through the
wilderness.

You may smile at first when your journey is compared to
this, because the only real "wilderness experience" most
of us ever know is our view of it from a motel room in Palm
Springs. The desert is a perfect place to winter when the
wild flowers are in blossom. There is nothing more spectacular than a desert sunrise when the entire world turns
red and yellow and purple, especially when the sunrise is
seen over a room-service breakfast in bed. But in the sands
just beneath the swimming pools and the air-conditioned
restaurants are the bones of the pioneers who traveled here
first.

That same desert was for them a place of horror and
hopelessness. They watched their children perish from
thirst and their wives go mad in the relentless desert sun.
Our forefathers saw many dreams die in the desert. Now
golf courses, million-dollar homes, and drive-in theaters
stand over their unmarked graves. Death Valley has become a vacation park, and people go to the desert to escape
the wilderness of the city—where some modern pioneers
watch their children die and their husbands or wives go
mad. The wilderness where you and I live may be air-
conditioned, but it is wilderness all the same.

One Saturday afternoon I sat behind a casket of a
longtime member of our church. The building was packed,

and at the close of the memorial service hundreds of our families filed by to pay their last respects to the deceased and his survivors. I looked into the faces of my congregation as they passed by that scene of death. It was the first time I had ever sat silently to watch them all walk by. As each family approached the coffin, paused, then moved on, I thought about the problems and the pain in their lives. I know the awful, ugly things that happen to them during the rest of the week. Each one is on a private, painful pilgrimage through a personal wilderness. Each of them struggles, as you and I struggle.

It doesn't take visiting Times Square or North Beach or Sunset Boulevard to see that life is a special wilderness for those who struggle with sexual lust. Television, motion pictures, magazine racks, singles bars, massage parlors, commercial advertisements, clothing styles, T-shirt messages, bumper stickers, cartoons, "the yellow pages," sex shops, or just a chance walk in certain parts of town may become a desert where one suddenly discovers himself or herself in a desperate struggle with sexual lust.

My own parishioners scold me when I talk about life as a journey through the wilderness. "Be more positive," they chide me. "Mel must have had a bad week," they whisper. "He's all gloom and doom again this morning." But you don't have to be a pessimist to see life as a wilderness. In fact, for Jesus the desert became a scene of great triumph. However, He didn't win out there in the heat and thirst and desolation by saying over and over to Himself, "I am having a wonderful time. Life isn't so difficult. This desert wandering is kind of fun." He suffered and struggled out there as we do. So we must go back two thousand years to remember His temptation in the desert in order to find help in our own struggles with sexual lust.

We Are Not Alone in the Wilderness

Picture Jesus walking in the desert. By all appearances He was alone. He cast only one shadow; He made only one set of footprints in the sand. Only one cloud of dust marked the place where Jesus passed, yet the Word assured us that He was not alone.

All three of the first-century witnesses (Matthew, Mark, and Luke) report that two other persons were present in the desert with Him: Satan and the Spirit (of God). Call them forces or powers or essences if it makes you feel better, but remember that whatever you call them, they are real. Satan and the Spirit are not simply the authors' attempts to dramatize two sides of Jesus' personality. They are not just two dimensions of a moral issue or two ways to answer the ethical questions which Jesus asked. Both Satan and the Spirit are real.

They work on human personality from inside and from outside the person. Modern readers of this story have a tendency to oversimplify the problem in one of two ways. A zealot may blame "the devil" for his or her own unethical acts. Blaming this other force is a way to wiggle out of one's own responsibility. A sceptic, on the other hand, refuses to believe that the devil and the Spirit even exist. These ancient notions, the sceptic reasons, are just ways to escape responsibility for our acts.

The first-century believers lived out a third option. They saw themselves, as Jesus saw Himself, as a battlefield where these two enemies—Satan and the Spirit of God— wage war, yet they equally admitted their own responsibility for deciding who would win the war. There are cases in the Old and New Testament of men and women who were taken over or possessed by Satan or "evil spirits," but these were extreme exceptions and not the rule. On the other hand, the believers after Pentecost were neither transformed into puppets by the presence of the Spirit in their lives, nor absolved of responsible decision making. They continued to be responsible to decide between the leadings of Satan or the Spirit.

We Will Face Temptation in the Wilderness

We must decide between good and evil. Jesus and His followers taught that Satan would enslave us, but God's Spirit would set us free. Satan works for our death and destruction; the Spirit works to give us life and health. Temptation is that point where the opposing desires of these two powers meet in our lives. The struggle point is a wilderness or desert through which we wander. Everybody has his or her own struggle points, his or her own deserts to cross. No one is miraculously exempted from the struggle.

There were no miracles out there for Jesus during His struggle with temptation. He promised us no miracles in our struggle with sex and lust, either. Beware the easy, instant answers from the beaming professional counselors who exorcise lust-guilt at fifty dollars an hour—or from those late-night television healers, hands stretched heavenward, who announce in piercing tones: "Someone out there in videoland is being healed of sexual lust. Praise Jesus!" Both extremes may forget Jesus' temptation and refuse to admit their own.

It doesn't take much backstage experience to discover that all our modern, media-made religious heroes and heroines face temptation just as we face it. All the big-name pastors, evangelists, teachers, and musicians leave the auditorium or the television studio and return to homes or hotels to face temptation like the rest of us. Beware those who deny it.

All the happy-ever-after conversions or other spiritual life stories must be read in light of the continuing temptation of their authors. Perhaps they are silent about their daily struggles because they know their audiences will quit buying, turn them off, or whisper in their ears, "I like it better when you tell about the miracle than when you talk about the temptations."

So—all miracle stories to the contrary—we cannot escape our time of temptation in the desert. We cannot think or entertain it away. We cannot even pray or praise it away. Neither can we move away to the suburbs or another state or nation in hopes that the temptation won't find us there. Wherever we go, whatever we do there, be sure that temptation will find us.

The problem is in remembering the larger significance of the private struggle with sexual lust. Some of us may minimize our struggles, hide them, or ignore them and hope they will go away. "This can't be happening to me," we gasp. "I'm one of the good guys. I'm a Christian and I'm supposed to be saved from all of that. I've been born again, filled with His Spirit. I can't be struggling still."

Oh, yes, you can be struggling still. Our story makes it perfectly clear. "Jesus, filled with the Holy Spirit, was tempted by the devil." Religious commitments or experiences do not remove us from the struggle. As long as we live we will fight temptation (sexual or otherwise). That "little problem" we have (that "little temptation" we are hiding) is in reality no little thing at all. It is the place where Satan is working to destroy us and God's dream for us, and we had better take our struggle seriously.

Others of us laugh off this idea of a war waged in our lives between God's Spirit and Satan. We buy into the modern notion that there aren't that many choices we actually can make. Our roots predetermine our fruits. Can a cabbage help being a cabbage? Does a mosquito feel guilt? Modern science often compares us to vegetables, insects, or machines. "We can't really make 'moral' decisions," some claim. "There are no universal standards of right and wrong, anyway. If it feels good, do it." Wrong!

Temptation is a battleground. Jesus' lonely stroll through the desert is described as a scene of battle in the timeless war between the superpowers of good and evil. That is the way Jesus pictured His temptation. (How else would the first-century writers have gotten the details?) And if Jesus saw His temptation as the place where Satan and God's Spirit wage war, why shouldn't I see my temptations in the same eternal light?

It helps me to remember, when I struggle with sexual lust or any other temptation, that there is a war going on. I am neither a vegetable, a machine, nor an accidental merging of sperm and egg. I am someone special whom God made, knows, and cares about. I am His child and He has dreams for me and for my life, as I have dreams for my daughter, Erin, and my son, Michael. The temptations which I face signal that Satan is at work to destroy God's dreams for me. It helps me to regain perspective when I remember that, though a particular enticement may seem harmless, it is in reality one more battle in a lifelong war that God is waging for me.

When You Are Tempted . . .

1. God's Word can help you. Feed on it! But let's get on with the story. What did Jesus do out there in the desert to win His war with Satan's first temptation? Picture Him walking in the endless wilderness. His skin is burned and peeling. His feet are raw and blistered. His body aches from sleeping on the rocky ground. His throat is caked with dust and He longs for something cool to drink. His stomach groans in hunger.

Because He was fasting, Jesus was not carrying any food or water on this journey. From early Jewish history we learn that the people of God went without eating or drinking, in order to excite God's pity and compassion in moments of distress or sorrow. David fasted during the illness of his and Bathsheba's first child, to gain God's sympathy for the dying infant. The Jews often fasted and prayed during times of intense national emergency or personal struggle, to convince God that their prayers were sincere. To spend time on daily trivia—cooking, eating, and doing dishes—would interrupt the process and show the people's insincerity. Fasting allowed a total focus on communicating with God.

Jesus had been fasting for forty days and nights as He communicated with God in the wilderness. At the moment when Jesus was most famished, the first temptation struck: "The tempter approached him," reads the ancient story, "and said, 'If you are the Son of God, tell these stones to become bread' " (Matthew 4:3).

Did Jesus stare for one brief moment at the flat, loaflike rocks of the desert? Did he remember the early-morning smells of his mother's fresh-baked bread and long for just one piece to eat? Days from now He would turn water into wine to save the host of a wedding feast from embarrassment. What could be wrong with turning rocks to bread in order to save His life and prove His power?

It was then that His Friend and Ally, the Holy Spirit, reminded Him of another wilderness a thousand years before. Moses was leading the people on their journey to the Promised Land. They, too, had blistered feet and dry throats. Their stomachs groaned for bread. And they howled their anger at Moses. "Take us back to Egypt," they complained. "We may have been slaves, but at least we weren't hungry."

Little did they know of God's plan for them in the desert. They did not realize that God was training them out there to be His people, teaching them to trust Him, to depend on Him. Later Moses explained to them, "God let you be hungry—to teach you that men cannot live by bread alone but by every word that comes from the mouth of God" (*see* Deuteronomy 8:3 KJV).

When the people complained, God heard them and fed them. In the morning, frosty flakes, white and sweet as honey, covered the ground. "Manna," they called it, eating joyfully. "Don't store it up," God warned, "for every day I will provide your needs." Even then God was teaching His people the pattern of trust. He was proving there at the beginning that they didn't need to worry. They could depend on Him. They didn't need to waste the power He had given them, just to meet their physical needs. God would be faithful.

Ancient Israelites and moderns know how quickly we forget to trust Him for our daily needs and waste the time bogged down in satisfying our hungers for food or water (or sex). Jesus looked the tempter in the face and quoted from the ancient story of manna in the wilderness: "Man cannot live on bread alone; he lives on every word that God utters" (Matthew 4:4).

It is the first lesson in the desert. Trust God. He will meet your needs. He will sustain you. If you go about His business and keep on His journey, your physical needs, including the sexual ones, will be taken care of by Him who made you, who understands you, and who loves you as He

loved His Son who struggled in the wilderness that hot,
hungry day.

2. God's Spirit is with you. Believe it!   Satan lost the first
round to the Holy Spirit. Jesus did not give in to the physical temptation. Now the more subtle struggle began. For
the second temptation the setting changed from the country
to the city. The devil's tactics changed as well. Now he
would quote the Scriptures first.

They stood together on a high wall above the temple
grounds in the Holy City of Jerusalem. Satan whispered to
Jesus, "If you are the Son of God . . . throw yourself
down; for Scripture says, 'He will put his angels in charge
of you, and they will support you in their arms, for fear you
should strike your foot against a stone' " (Matthew 4:6).

Again the Holy Spirit caused Jesus to remember His ancestors' first journey across the wilderness. They had seen
God meet their needs with miracles: the plagues, the open-
ing of the Red Sea, the manna from heaven. Still they did
not trust Him. So, when they grew thirsty, they rioted
again. They shouted at Moses: "Did you bring us to the
desert so that we and our cattle might die of thirst?"

And Moses answered, "Why do you tempt the Lord?"
The people had seen God work, but the minute the manna
was gone, they forgot the miracle and doubted His promise
to provide. So Moses cried out to God, "The people don't
believe You travel with us. They cannot see You and so
they think they journey alone. What shall we do?"

God in His faithfulness instructed Moses to assemble the
people and strike a rock with his staff. Water poured from
that rock and again God met His people's needs as He had
promised. But God was not pleased with the people's lack
of faith. He was not happy that they needed miracle after
miracle to prove Him in their midst. So He had Moses name

the site of that miracle *Massah* (which means the place of testing or temptation) and *Meribah* (the place where the people chided God).

God is distressed with our abiding urge to wait until we are sure. For we will never be sure enough. There can never be enough proof to take away the necessary element of faith. In spite of all God's gifts, there never seems to be sufficient evidence for some to trust Him. So man goes on testing his Creator, waiting to be sure that God is traveling with him, and thus never begins the journey.

God does not approve this ancient cycle of testing. He longs for us to get on with our journey. He cries out across the ages, "Don't doubt Me. Go on believing that I am with you, miracle or no miracle. Besides," He reminds us, "I give you a miracle, and two seconds later you forget it and demand another. Your journey is by faith. Move out! Follow Me. And when the journey ends, you will look back and you will realize I was with you every step along the way. Quit stalling!" God calls us: "Quit interrupting the journey. Quit looking for miracles. Quit tempting Me."

Satan was tempting God in the same way when he asked Jesus, "How do You know You are not alone out here? How can You be sure that God will meet His promises and care for You unless You test Him? Jump off this building, and if the angels catch You before You stub Your little toe, we will know for certain." And Jesus answered Satan with the same words Moses used against the people: ". . .You are not to put the Lord your God to the test" (Matthew 4:7). When you long for a miracle in your own struggle with temptation, remember; "You are not to test the Lord." Go on trusting Him. He will be faithful.

3. God's will is best for you. Do it! Now Satan was getting desperate. For the second time he had lost the battle.

He walked silently beside his intended victim to the top of a mountain with a clear view of the world. Before this third temptation, Satan stood beside Jesus, watching Him for any sign of weakness. Jesus must have been near exhaustion now. He stared down at all those things which have dazzled and distracted men and women from the beginning.

What would tempt Jesus? Palaces, harems, honor, guards, wealth, power, privilege, prestige? Perhaps the simpler things could lure Him away: the glory of a warm meal, a soft bed and a tender, loving body in that bed beside Him?

"Look," Satan might have whispered grudgingly, "You've proven Your faithfulness to Your Father. You've shown that He has set Your course, and I can't keep You from it. But, Jesus, how much can He ask of You? After all that You've been through, even God would not blame You for taking a night off.

"I'll tell You what I'll do. Whatever You want down there, I will give You. Whatever fantasy has ever crossed Your mind is Yours. Just forget Him for this one brief moment. Just ignore Him and spend the night with me. Then, in the morning, quick as a wink, You can go back to Him again. Probably no one will ever know. Give me a little respect [disobey just this once] and I will give You the world."

Again the Holy Spirit came to Jesus' aid. He remembered what His people learned on their wilderness journey. What may look like a "night off" is in reality the beginning of disobedience. We quit obeying God. We quit following Him and worship another.

The ancient Jews took time off when Moses was delayed on Mount Sinai. They gave in to their tiredness from the journey. They gave in to the standards of their pagan neighbors. On their night off they built a golden calf and danced around it in a drunken orgy. And Moses, trembling in rage, returned to smash the covenant Commandments, ground the calf into powder, cast the powder on the water, and made the people drink it. Three thousand of them died that night as a lesson to all of us who wonder about "a night off for disobedience," a "time out for unfaithfulness."

So Jesus, remembering, quoted again from that ancient story: "Go away, Satan, for Scripture says, 'You shall worship the Lord your God and Him alone.' " (*See* Deuteronomy 6:13 and Matthew 4:10.)

It was then that Satan, the spirit of evil, left Him. He would return to tempt Jesus again. Even the night before His Crucifixion, Jesus struggled in the garden with the tempter. That last night He spent with His disciples before His death, Jesus warned them, "Watch and pray, that ye enter not into temptation: the spirit indeed is willing, but the flesh is weak" (Matthew 26:41 KJV). Jesus was tempted throughout His lifetime, and so will we be tempted. But Jesus was not alone in His temptation. The Holy Spirit was with Him as He is with us when we are tempted. And because of the Holy Spirit's presence, Jesus conquered His temptations. And so can we.

Remember how the wilderness story ends? After three temptations the Evil One left Jesus. Immediately, God sent messengers to wait on His faithful Son. When we are tempted, not only will the Holy Spirit be there with us, but when the temptations end, God will also meet our needs.

SUMMARY

Story 5: Jesus' Temptation in the Wilderness
(How Should I Respond to My Own Sexual Lust?)

Jesus was tempted by sexual lust, as we are tempted (*see* Hebrews 4:15, 16). Compare His struggle with temptation to our struggle:

1. Life can be a wilderness (a hostile, alien environment).
2. We are not alone in the wilderness (both the Spirit of God and the spirit of evil are with us).
3. Temptation is the time and place where these two powers collide in our lives (where God and the Evil One struggle against each other for our love and loyalty).

Jesus survived His struggle with temptation. From His victory we can learn solutions to our own struggle with sexual lust and all kinds of temptation.

1. When you are tempted, *God's Word can help you.* Feed on it!
2. When you are tempted, *God's Spirit is with you.* Believe it!
3. When you are tempted, *God's will is best for you.* Do it!

Matthew 4:1–11   The Temptation Story
Luke 4:1–13

Story 6

JESUS
AND THE ADULTEROUS WOMAN
(How Should I Respond to Sexual Lust in Others?)

At this moment there is a fiercely pitched battle being waged by some of my evangelical brothers and sisters against equal-rights laws for homosexuals. I am not writing to campaign for either side. We all must do our homework prayerfully and decide carefully on this issue. What troubles me is the apparent growing hatred and fear which I feel being directed against the homosexual, as though he or she were more guilty of sexual lust than the heterosexual struggler. Didn't Jesus Himself establish our mutual guilt in His Sermon on the Mount? (*See* Matthew 5:27–48.)

Some well-known evangelical leaders have been quoted in the press as having said, "Gays are garbage." Or, "Homosexuality is a sin so low, so rotten, so dirty that even cats and dogs don't practice it." Or even, "So-called gay folks would just as soon kill you as look at you."

I am sure that many of these ugly, untrue statements have been taken out of context in the heat of campaign rhetoric. Surely, most of them have been exaggerated and even misquoted by the press. For, if not, the church people saying those things make us all look like the Pharisee in Jesus' parable (*see* Luke 18:1–14).

One wag, picking up the apparent evangelical attitude, printed a tongue-in-cheek bumper sticker (now appearing on cars in our neighborhood) with this ugly statement: KILL A QUEER FORCHRIST.

The critic who printed the sticker perceived church people as holding up the Bible in one hand and waving a finger of condemnation with the other. In our struggle to do right, some of us have made the body of Christ look self-righteous, judgmental, hypocritical, and aloof. By retelling the story of Sodom and leaving untold the story of Jesus with the adulterous woman, we may keep alive the false notion of an angry, unloving God of law and forget His loving Son Jesus, who fulfilled that law and gave lawbreakers the chance to begin again.

Do you remember that dramatic story from His life, as told in John 8:1–11, when a woman caught in the act of adultery was dragged through the crowd by the Pharisees and dropped at Jesus' feet? Although it is more likely the homosexual being dragged through today's crowd, Jesus taught us through His response to the adulterous woman how we should respond to any kind of sexual immorality in others. Picture it!

How the Pharisees Responded to Sexual Lust in Others (One Quick Step to Judgment)

It was early morning in the ancient city of Jerusalem. The sunrise still glistened on the marble walls and pillared arches of Herod's temple. In the courtyard hundreds of people were gathering to hear Jesus teach them from the Scriptures. He had just taken His seat to begin telling them a parable of the Kingdom, when suddenly a handful of Pharisees and doctors of the law pushed their way to the front of the startled crowd.

These religious leaders with their long robes and colorful

sashes of authority were the official Jewish Bible teachers. They prided themselves on their discovery of 613 different commandments in Mosaic Law. In public they loved to quote, interpret, and enforce their 248 positive and 365 negative commands. They were quick to condemn anyone who broke these laws or their own official interpretations of them.

That morning they had trapped a young woman in the act of adultery. They dragged her to the temple courtyard and deposited her at Jesus' feet. Loudly they shouted above the noise of the crowd, "Master, this woman was caught in the very act of adultery." The people stared at the frightened woman cringing in the middle of the Pharisees. She tried to escape her shame by falling to the ground. The persecutors' strong hands forced her to her feet again.

She had good reason to be afraid. Even then, one of the Pharisees was loudly reminding, "The Law of Moses has laid down that such women are to be stoned." His was no empty threat. Although this particular punishment for adultery was two thousand years old and given when God's primitive people had forgotten Him in an orgy of disobedience, it was still on the books. (It still is. Read it in your own Bible: Leviticus 20:10.) And though this punishment was not generally enforced in Jesus' day—as it is not enforced in our day—the Pharisees carried stones to obey the law literally and thus execute her on the spot.

Actually, they were after Jesus not the woman. She was only the bait in their trap to dishonor and discredit this young teacher. He had threatened their stranglehold on the people with His loving interpretation of the law. Jesus was not soft on sin. He taught and obeyed the law. But He also knew the loving heart of God behind the law. God had given the law to *help* His people, not to hurt them. God used the law to guide His people in their relationships with each other and with Him, not to trap and condemn them as did the Pharisees.

These proud men waved the law with one hand and pointed their finger of judgment with the other. They insisted that the people keep all the law—while they themselves often disobeyed it, quoted it out of context, used it to their own advantage, and ignored portions of it when necessary. They may have known the words of the law by memory, but they had long since forgotten God's reason for giving the law. He meant the law to lead the people to life. In the Pharisees' hands the law became an instrument of death.

The woman had sinned. She must die. It was an open-and-closed case to them. So they rushed to judge her. She would be a lesson to the people and a means to destroy Jesus' growing influence. After all, He had said: "I have come to fulfill the law, not to destroy it." Now they had Him trapped with the same law He promised to fulfill.

If He disobeyed the law in the very shadow of the temple, they could rend their robes in mock horror and discredit His teaching forever. But if He obeyed the law, picked up a heavy stone, and knocked the brains out of this poor, helpless woman, the people would turn from Him in horror and fear.

The crowd buzzed with excitement. Wide-eyed with terror and suspense, the woman looked at Jesus. Her life was in His hands now.

How Jesus Responded to Sexual Lust in Others
(Four Slow Steps to Mercy)

In the great temple courtyard, pilgrims, priests, and merchants stood stock-still. Every eye was focused on Jesus. The only sounds to be heard were the quiet sobs of the woman trembling at His feet and the whispered demands of the Pharisees: "What will You do with this woman caught in the act of adultery?" An eyewitness, John the disciple, reports that Jesus said nothing. Instead, He paused, bent down, and wrote something on the ground.

Step One: Jesus Paused

Let Jesus' pause always be our first reply to another's sinfulness. It is easy to rush to judgment. But the road to mercy is a slow and painful journey. We don't really know what Jesus wrote on the ground that day. And we have no record of what went through His mind. But we can know from Jesus' life and teachings what He must have been concerned about as He paused before responding to her sexual lust.

He was concerned about the sin. After all, He had told them many times that He had come not to destroy the law but to complete its purpose. Of course, He couldn't just ignore the broken law out of pity for the woman. Adultery is a grave matter. And she was guilty without question. If He just smiled and sent her away, He would be implying to the people that God isn't really serious about His warnings against adultery (or any other command, for that matter). And He knew well that God *was* serious about adultery and its long-range damage to His children.

But He also knew that the Pharisees were misusing this law and its ancient penalty to get what they wanted and not simply to preserve the truth. The instant death penalty for adultery had been given two thousand years before when the Israelites were a motley crowd of feuding ex-slave families on a journey through the wilderness. God had formed this infant people to rescue the world. But their journey to His dream for them bogged down in a heathen land. God's people ignored His laws in an orgy of disobedience. They were even sacrificing infant children to the pagan god Molech. God was about to lose His people and with them His dream to rescue the world.

How many times have we heard the story of a mother who notices her child about to run into a busy street! From the house the mother screams her warnings: "No! Spank!" The danger is too imminent and the child is too young and too naive to be given reasons. Only a loud, quick threat of punishment can save him from a serious accident.

This ancient passage was God's loud threat to His infant nation. They were about to destroy themselves—and the danger was too imminent, the nation too young and too naive for reasons. They were not taking His warnings seriously. They were letting pagan neighbors set their moral standards—and God got angry. He cried out one more warning threat. In the temple courtyard that day, two thousand years later, the Pharisees quoted that same threat (Leviticus 20:10), without remembering when and why God made it.

It is interesting to note that in 1692 the witch-hunters of Salem, Massachusetts, quoted from the same chapter in the same ancient book (Leviticus 20:27), to support the torture and hanging of their victims. Christians today are quoting from the same chapter in the same ancient book to support their angry cries against the homosexual. These ancient laws from Leviticus require that if a man "lie with mankind [another man]" he be put to death (v. 13 KJV), but they require a child who swears at his parent to be put to death as well (*see* v. 9). The same chapter requires a couple who has sexual intercourse during the woman's menstrual period to "be cut off from among their people" (*see* v. 18 KJV).

Don't misunderstand me. God has not changed His mind about adultery, witchcraft, or homosexuality. These practices are still roads that lead away from God and to our destruction and to the death of His dream for us. But four thousand years have passed. The people of God should be old enough by now to understand that, though the old law still provides a valid and serious warning, the penalty for breaking that law has been paid by God Himself. And though the edicts still stand in Leviticus, we have the Gospels to help us understand and apply them.

In a later chapter we will recall the dramatic climax to Jesus' life. We will see again how He has fulfilled (or satisfied or taken on Himself) our penalty for disobeying the law. But Jesus' arrest, trial, and crucifixion were still months away. In His response to the woman's lust, He is about to make clear by His life—as He will make even clearer by His death—how far our loving Father will go to rescue us, even when we ignore His warnings and disobey.

Remember the mother who screamed her threat of punishment to keep her child from running into the street? If the child ignored the warnings, disobeyed, and was hurt anyway, the mother cried out for her child's pain and rushed to save the one she loved from his self-inflicted suffering. Jesus is not soft on sin. He is not about to ignore the ancient penalty prescribed by the law, out of sentimental or thoughtless pity. He is about to demonstrate the loving heart of God behind the laws against sin and rush to save the sinner.

He was concerned about the sinner.   To the Pharisees, the woman sobbing at Jesus' feet was just another whore. In those ancient times, a woman had few rights and a prostitute had none. Men held the superior and privileged place. (Perhaps that is why no *man* lay trembling with guilt beside the woman at Jesus' feet; even though Leviticus 20:10

states clearly that the woman *and the man* who commit adultery are to be stoned.)

No one in the crowd that day caught the Pharisees breaking one law to keep another. (By the way, a few verses earlier (19:18), any thinking member of that courtyard crowd could have found another ancient law which the Pharisees ignored: "Thou shalt love thy neighbour as thyself." This command to love was verses older than the other command which the Pharisees quoted that day. The "law of love" wasn't original with Jesus.) But these Pharisees, like modern hypocrites, chose one law over another, misquoted that law, and sacrificed the lawbreaker to get what they wanted. They could use this woman to bait their deadly trap because, although they quoted Scripture, they didn't understand or reflect the heart of God behind His Word.

Jesus understood that God loved the lawbreaker and meant the law to save this adulteress by guiding her in her relationships, human and divine. He saw that woman, tearstained and trembling on the ground, not as a worthless whore but as a priceless child of God. He loved her as God loved her. Jesus understood that she was not the only one to blame. She was a victim of her past, of her culture—and now, because of the Pharisees' misuse of the law, a victim of even her religion.

He knew that the trail that leads a victim to disobedience and to death is complex and lifelong. There are forces in every person's life that he or she did not choose and does not understand. What a mother-to-be does to damage herself may also damage the infant. Evil may do its work before a child's birth. Evil may work in the hospital those first hours after birth. Improper diet may damage the brain. Excessive oxygen may blind the eyes. Inadequate space may cripple the body. Evil works in early childhood and adolescence—shaping the child through parents, friends, neighbors and neighborhoods, natural disasters, wars, personal tragedies, crime, home environment, weather, disease, stress, and countless other visible and invisible forces.

Like adultery, homosexual practices have been clearly marked in Scripture as dangerous and destructive. However, before we rush to condemn the homosexual's lust, let us at least pause to remember the complex forces that may have shaped the homosexual person from childhood.

We know that millions of people may be sexually aroused by members of the same sex through no fault of their own. Though each of us is responsible for his or her sexual behavior, we must pause before we blame each other for our sexual preference. There are other evil forces in and around us, twisting and distorting all of God's Creation. As one desperate Christian who has fought his homosexuality from childhood said to me, "I didn't ask to be a homosexual. I didn't want to be so shaped. I would give anything if it had never happened."

Evil shapes and affects us from our beginnings. So when someone else is dragged before us by his or her accusers, it is best we pause, as Jesus paused, to love and understand that person as much as He loved the adulteress that day two thousand years ago.

Step Two: Jesus Reminded the Accusers of Their Own Sexual Lust

Jesus' long pause only caused the Pharisees to press their questions harder: "This woman has broken the law. The penalty is clear. She must die. What do You say about it?" Suddenly He sat up straight and looked at her accusers:

"That one of you who is faultless shall throw the first stone." Then Jesus bent down again and continued writing on the ground.

I wish I could have been there that moment, when in one short sentence He settled forever the question of our attitude toward another person's failures. I wish I could have seen the look on the faces of the doctors of the law as they were caught in their own trap by the brilliance of His reply. I wish I could have seen the joyful surprise in the woman's eyes as those heavy stones slid from their hands, and one by one her accusers disappeared into the crowd.

But before I cheer His victory and their defeat too smugly, I must remember that it was no small act of courage for them to drop those rocks and walk away. For in that act the official keepers of the law confessed before the people that they, too, were lawbreakers. In a similar jam, I wonder if modern Pharisees might not have stoned her.

Similarly, as a few angry church people deliver their accusations against homosexuals, it may be their brothers and sisters in Christ who are hurt the most. Every church has some members who struggle secretly with homosexual lust. Through the Spirit of God and the fellowship of compassionate believers, many of these same strugglers have seen slow but certain victories in their lives. But just as often, a thoughtless Christian may be the cause of a brother's or sister's secret agony.

A speaker who spits out his contempt at homosexuality may drive a secret struggler further into loneliness and despair. The thoughtless comments by Christian parents, unaware that their own child may be afflicted with homosexual tendencies, can drive the suffering one further into isolation. Church members, often guilty of heterosexual lust themselves, may make tasteless jokes or snide remarks about homosexuals and thoughtlessly dehumanize and demean the brothers and sisters who struggle beside them. When will we learn the meaning of Jesus' words to the Pharisees that day: "That one of you who is faultless shall throw the first stone."? When will we let the stones of judgment fall from our hands in order to reach out in love to our fellow sinners? He was forcing them (and us) to remember our own sinfulness. When we feel the urge to comment on another person's sinfulness, we should preface our remarks with: "Brothers and sisters, I, too, am a sinner. I, too, am guilty." Then we can quote Scripture. Then we can campaign and take stands. For then we are kneeling on the ground beside our fellow accused—and no longer standing over them in judgment. They will know the difference.

Step Three: Jesus Refused to Condemn

The eyewitness reports that one by one her accusers went away. "Convicted by their own conscience," realizing their own guilt, the Pharisees quit condemning her and disappeared into the crowd. It is interesting to note that John reports that they left "beginning at the eldest" (*see* John 8:9 KJV).

When I was a teenager, one of my father's friends was murdered in a hotel room in New York. Later we learned that he had hired a young male prostitute for violent sex acts and had accidentally been killed in the process. I couldn't believe then that this outstanding city official, much-loved husband and father, could have such an ugly, secret side. I remember wondering, "How could anyone like him stoop so low?"

It was easy to condemn when I was young. The rapist, the incestuous parent, the prostitute, the lone killer who murdered as a sexual act—or the poor city father who stumbled in a distant city and died in shame—were easy to judge in those days. Now two decades have passed. I find it difficult to condemn, for now I have spent long, lonely nights in hotel rooms myself. I have walked the streets of New York and Paris and Hong Kong. I have discovered that—given the wrong set of circumstances—I, too, am vulnerable to sexual lust.

I used to be shocked and surprised by the variety of lust I heard confessed by my Christian brothers and sisters. Now, no new variation on the sexual theme can surprise or shock me. What I find difficult to believe is how well we hide our sexual-lust side from each other. And worse, how quickly even the most guilty of us can condemn another!

At least the Pharisees could still hear their consciences. At least the adulterous woman's accusers had the good sense to go away and leave her alone with Jesus. Remember, He was the only one in the crowd that day who had the right to stone her. For Jesus, though tempted like the rest of them, had not given in to temptation. He was not guilty—so He *could* have thrown the first stone. He could condemn her with impunity. But He didn't.

She stood alone before Him. The last Pharisee had gone. Suddenly Jesus sat up for the second time.

"Where are they?" He asked her. "Has no one condemned you?"

Perhaps it was at that moment when she first realized they were gone. "No one, sir," she answered in relief.

"Neither do I condemn thee . . ." He answered (John 8:11 KJV).

Suddenly we remember Jesus, earlier in His life, telling the Pharisee Nicodemus: "For God sent not his Son into the world to condemn the world; but that the world through him might be saved" (John 3:17 KJV). Why can't we remember His words and His example in our relationships with other people? If Jesus, the perfect Man, refused to condemn that woman, why is it so easy for us, *who are imperfect,* to condemn those like her?

Jesus never condemned the Romans for their pagan gods and their immoral standards. The only people Jesus did condemn were the Pharisees. Now we use their name to describe the hypocritical, sanctimonious, and self-righteous person. And He condemned the Pharisees—not for their sins, but for refusing to admit their own sins while condemning the sins of others.

In fact, we have specific New Testament instructions *not* to condemn the unbeliever. The Apostle Paul wrote, "What business of mine is it to judge outsiders? God is their judge . . ." (1 Corinthians 5:12). If Jesus judged only the self-righteous religious leaders and if Paul instructed us clearly to judge only "within the fellowship," then why are we modern Christians tempted to decide for a nonbeliever what his or her moral standards should be? What right have we to legislate any nonbeliever's morality? According to Scripture, we have no such right or responsibility!

People ask, "What happens when a person is caught red-handed? What should we do when someone flaunts his sexual lust or continues stubbornly in it? Must we stand helplessly by as the struggler continues to destroy himself and brings danger and damage to others?" Must we be silent while another models sinfulness to innocent children? Of course not! To refuse to condemn does not mean we must be naive, sentimental, silent, or cowardly in dealing with sexual lust in others.

Step Four: Jesus Warned Against Sin

The woman's accusers were gone. The rocks they had carried to kill her lay piled at the young rabbi's feet. And now even He refused to condemn her. It should have been a moment of great relief, but the woman was street-wise enough to know how much the public exposure would cost her. If she were a prostitute, as many suspect, this humiliation destroyed any hope she may have had for a secure future. Old clients would shun her to save their reputation, and no sane man would ever want her for his wife again. She would be known forever as "the woman caught in the act of adultery." Her life was ruined. She even may have wondered if it might have been more merciful to stone her.

Then Jesus spoke to her one last time: ". . . go, and sin no more" (John 8:11 KJV). I imagine that the people in the crowd who knew her reputation barely stifled their laughter when He told the prostitute to *go, and sin no more*. In their eyes (and probably in her own eyes) she was a hopeless case. She was shaped by her past, molded by her history, her bad choices, her culture, her vocation, and her reputation in a vicious cycle of sexual lust. Everyone in that crowd knew that "once you get that far down there is no way up again." You might as well stone her as to ask her to quit sinning.

On the other hand, Jesus knew it would have been so much easier to let her off the hook with His words—*I don't condemn you*. The crowd would have cheered His being soft on sin, especially in her unfortunate case. She was a victim. She had suffered enough. "Go easy on her. Leave her in her misery." But soft, sentimental mercy is as bad as no mercy at all. Mercy has its difficult, demanding side. And He cared enough to go all the way with her on the road to mercy. "Go, and sin no more," He said.

He called it sin. Jesus didn't wink at her adultery or excuse it with an easy alibi. He didn't ignore it, nor did He jump up and down hysterically in the face of it, as did the Pharisees. He called her sexual lust by its proper name—*sin.*

To many moderns until recently, the word *sin* seemed so old-fashioned and inadequate a label. Now one of America's leading psychiatrists, Dr. Karl Menninger, in his book *Whatever Became of Sin?,* advises that unless we rediscover and admit to sin again we have no way to rid ourselves of guilt and self-hatred. Until we call it sin, we have no way to be forgiven.

In our dealings with those caught in sexual lust, mercy is incomplete unless we do as Jesus did: call it sin. We have winked and giggled, made alibis, or ignored sin all too long. A friend in need is one who says quietly but firmly, "What you're doing, friend, is sin. It is harmful to you and to others. It is destructive to God's dream for you."

He advised her to quit sinning. Sexual lust may look cute and innocent on the screen or in a lurid paperback, but in spite of its current popularity, it will destroy God's dream in us. He said it quietly but He said it, nevertheless: "Don't sin anymore."

We tend to feel self-righteous when we give another sinner advice. We like to be nondirective, supportive, good listeners. We hate to sound puritanical or judgmental. So we listen and love in the name of mercy, when we should also have the courage to say, "That is wrong. Quit doing it, for your own sake and others."

His words gave her hope. His invitation to "go, and sin no more" was an invitation to begin again. It was a sign of the incredible confidence He placed in her. It was a goal that she could carry in her heart forever. It was a guideline for every major decision she would make. He was not mocking her. It was His promise that she could do it.

After we have paused before another's sexual lust, after we have remembered our own guilt and refused to condemn the guilt of another, then we must say with Jesus, "Now go—and sin no more." Otherwise, our mercy is incomplete.

Picture how that ugly confrontation may have ended. . . . For a moment she stared at Him. Since her youth she had heard similar words from her parents, the priests, and the Pharisees. "Don't be a bad little girl." "Don't do this!" "Don't do that." "Shame!" "Naughty! Naughty!" They spoke to condemn her. But He had just said, "I don't condemn you." Something about His last words—"Go, and sin no more"—made her feel hope again.

It was crazy. As she retreated into the shadowed corridors of the temple and raced down the marble steps to the safety of the crowds below, His words echoed in her brain. "Go, and sin no more." How could those five words make her heart beat with excitement and her feet dance with joy?

For years she may have lurked about those same busy streets, emerging from the shadows to tempt young men whose purses jingled—and then retreating back into the shadows to hide from those who condemned and pursued her. Now His words sent her singing through the streets, as though she were a little girl again and alive with hope. It was as though she had been born again.

And all He had said to her was: "I don't condemn you. Go, and sin no more." *All?* What else do we need to hear to give us hope again? *I don't condemn you* means you have another chance. Go for it. It means you can make the hard decisions. "I believe in you. Whoever you are, you *can* begin again. And if you fail, I will forgive you and see you safely home."

At a church conference grounds last summer, a young teenage counselor was accused of making sexual advances to one of the young counselees in his cabin. Panic ensued in the adult staff. One senior member insisted that the boy be fired and sent home immediately. (That would have been condemnation in the spirit of the Pharisees.) Another counselor who knew and liked the accused refused to deal with the issue at all and wanted the matter dropped. (That would have been naive and cowardly.)

The camp director met with the teenage counselor. For the first time in his life, the boy confessed his homosexual struggle. The camp director assured him that his feelings were common, though destructive, and convinced him that he was there to help and not condemn the boy. They talked and prayed together. The boy felt God's pardon and man's acceptance, as they worked together on an immediate and long-range solution to his problem.

The director asked the boy to move into a staff cabin where seven other young adults were housed. The boy spent the remaining days of camp working under supervision on trail maintenance, where he had no direct contact with the offended child. The young man agreed to meet regularly during the coming year with a trained professional in his church, and the director called the psychologist, with the boy's permission, to make the arrangements. In April of the following year the director met with the pastor and the Christian psychologist and determined that the teenager had made great progress. The boy was hired for the coming summer and given a supervised recreation job. That is where the matter stands.

It would have been a lot easier for the camp director to condemn the boy and send him home. Instead, he cared. There are no long-range guarantees for all the hours of work the director invested in that boy's life. But by every indication, his act of caring may have been the most significant and life-changing ministry which the director has ever had. He remembered Jesus' words: "I have come not to condemn but to rescue."

Jesus showed us how to respond to sexual lust in others, whether the homosexual, the unwed mother, the adulterer, or any other. I am convinced that His example can and must guide us. First, let us *pause* in the face of another's sexual lust. Let our voices grow quiet for one thoughtful moment. Let us consider not just the sin but the sinner. Second, let us *remember our own sexual lust,* confess it, and drop the stones of judgment that we carry. Third, let us *refuse to condemn others,* but give them the same chance which God and others have given us. And fourth, let us *gently and lovingly warn those who have given in to sexual lust* that it is sin and will lead to destruction and to death.

SUMMARY

Story 6: Jesus and the Adulterous Woman
(How Should I Respond to Sexual Lust in Others?)

One morning a woman caught in the act of adultery was dragged through the crowds by the Pharisees and dropped at Jesus' feet. In that moment Jesus taught us how to respond to sexual lust in others. His Four Slow Steps to Mercy should be our response to all those we know who fail in any area.

1. Pause before we respond.
2. Remember that we are guilty, too.
3. Refuse to condemn another.
4. Warn the accused to stop the harmful, destructive act.

John 8:1–11   The Story of Jesus and
                the Adulterous Woman

Story 7

JESUS, THE CROSS, AND THE EMPTY TOMB

(Will I Ever Win the Struggle With Sexual Lust?)

Jesus' words to the woman caught in adultery—"Go, and sin no more"—may have sent her dancing into the streets that day of her escape. But what happened in the days or months or years ahead when once again she gave in to the urge to yield to sexual temptation? Perhaps she was miraculously cured from the sexual lust of her past. We don't know how her story ends. What worries us is how *our* stories will end. For most of us there will be no miracle cure for temptation. And though His compassionate message—to begin again and sin no more—provides us with an exciting and rewarding goal, what happens if we fail? What will become of us if we lose our struggle against sexual lust? Will we end up in hell, lost forever?

The Apostle Paul scared members of the mission church in Corinth—and a lot of modern readers as well—with these words:

> . . . Make no mistake: no fornicator or idolater, none who are guilty either of adultery or of homosexual perversion . . . will possess the kingdom of God . . . .
>
> 1 Corinthians 6:9, 10

For centuries this passage has been misused by priests, parents, evangelists, ministers, and crusaders against sexual lust to maintain morality through fear. For those who have failed in their struggle against sexual temptations (or live in fear of failure) misunderstanding these words of Paul has been not only a deathblow to hope but a final source of alienation from God. But when we understand Paul's words correctly, they will give birth to new hope for God's people.

Readers of this ancient letter make a terrible mistake if they quit reading after discovering in shock and in horror that no adulterer or homosexual or fornicator can possess the Kingdom of God.

Read on! Paul continues immediately:

> And such were some of you [Adulterers, homosexuals, and fornicators were members of the Corinthian church.]: but ye are washed, but ye are sanctified, but ye are justified in the name of the Lord Jesus, and by the Spirit of our God.
>
> 1 Corinthians 6:11 KJV

In this ancient formula we find the answer to the pesky question that haunts us: "What happens if we fail in our struggle with temptation?" In Paul's three mysterious words—*washed, sanctified, justified*—we discover the source of the authentic Christian hope that is ours forever, whether we succeed or fail in our struggle to obey His command: "Go, and sin no more."

Moses, Passover, and the Sacrificial System

To understand the mystery, we go back two thousand years to the ancient city of Jerusalem. We remember the scene memorialized by Leonardo da Vinci's "Last Supper." Jesus was celebrating the Passover feast with His disciples. Judas had dipped into their much depleted treasury to buy the sacrificial lamb. The table was spread with unleavened bread, bitter herbs, and roast lamb, as it was first spread two thousand years before by Jesus' ancestors. This ancient feast had roots in Egypt when the Jews were still slaves in Pharaoh's brickworks.

The promised day of freedom had come. Moses assembled the elders and whispered God's instructions. His voice must have trembled with excitement as he told the people: "Sacrifice a perfect lamb. Splash its blood on the upper doorpost of your house. Then roast and eat the lamb with unleavened bread and bitter herbs. But eat with your shoes on your feet and your staff in your hand and eat in haste: It is the Lord's Passover." (*See* Exodus 12.)

That night the angel of death killed the firstborn sons of Egypt. Pharaoh had disobeyed God's servant. The Egyptian king had refused to let God's people go. So God plagued Pharaoh for his disobedience, but the people of God were spared because they did as they were told. The blood of the sacrificial lamb that they had spread on the doorposts of their homes signaled the angel of death to pass over and spare the people inside. From that night, Israelites have celebrated the Passover feast, a memorial to God's promised deliverance from death and slavery.

Jesus' New Sacrifice

Jesus and His disciples were about to celebrate the Passover. Before they could roast the lamb on a spit of pomegranate wood over a charcoal fire, it had to be taken to the temple for sacrifice. There priests in colorful robes, reciting prayers and singing ancient songs, killed the lamb, let its blood drain on the altar and portions of its flesh roast in the sacrificial fire as a sweet-smelling offering to God.

By Jesus' time, sacrifice had become a complex ritual at the heart of Jewish faith. Birds and animals, fruit and grain, and oil and spices were given to God in the temple on appointed feast days or as an act of thanksgiving, for tribute, for worship, or for forgiveness of sin.

As the sacrificial system evolved, the penalty for a person's guilt from breaking the Law of God could thereby be removed. The tainted body and mind could be reconditioned by the shed blood of a sacrifice dropped by a priest on the ear, thumb, and toe of the offerer—as prescribed in Exodus 29:20. Since the blood had been consecrated by its contact with God's altar, the procedure of washing with blood signaled the regeneration or rebirth of the guilty person, and the death sentence was removed. The guilty one was literally made alive again.

It is impossible for us to get inside those ancient Hebrew heads to really understand their sacrificial system. But we can know without a doubt that by Jesus' time, the temple, its priests, and their sacrifices had become a corrupt and exploitive system. Moneychangers short-changed and cheated the poor. Merchants charged Grade A prices for scrawny, sickly sacrificial animals. Priest and Sadducees increased their own wealth and power by demanding that the people buy their way to salvation.

The sins of priests and laymen increased until the sacrificial system, meant to alleviate sin, became a sin itself. The law condemned the people for their sinfulness but provided no way for their guilt to be removed. Jesus came to provide

God's new way of forgiveness.

That Last Supper night, as Jesus and His disciples were celebrating the *old* Passover feast, He announced God's new promise to His disciples. They had just finished eating the herbs and roasted lamb when suddenly the Master took a loaf of unleavened bread and began to pray over it. When His prayer ended, Jesus broke the bread and passed out pieces to the tongue-tied disciples.

"This is My body," He said. "Take and eat." They stared at the bread and then at Him. His words didn't make sense, but they obeyed and ate as He had told them. Then He took a cup of wine. "This is My blood," He announced, "of the new era [testament, covenant] which is shed for the forgiveness of sin. Drink you all of it."

The chalice passed up and down the table. Each man drank from Jesus' wine. Each man wondered what it could mean. How could His blood be shed for their forgiveness of sin? They didn't realize it then, but the old sacrificial system was dying before their eyes. He would be the New Sacrifice, the sufficient way for all people and all times to say to God, "I'm sorry." Through Him, old guilt would be removed forever and their lives made new again.

They sang a final hymn, walked down the steps into the darkness, and across the Brook Kidron to the Mount of Olives. Next to the quiet hills above Galilee, this was Jesus' favorite place to pray. They had often accompanied Him to this spot. Sitting up against the gnarled olive trees, they could see the silhouettes of the city and temple in the moonlight. Jerusalem was dark and quiet. In spite of Jesus' warnings, the disciples dozed.

What happened next seemed like a nightmare. Judas appeared in the darkness and kissed Jesus on the cheek. Tem-

ple guards rushed from hiding to arrest Him. There was a
quick scuffle; then He was gone. It all happened so fast: His
mock trial before the High Priests, His dialogue with the
Roman Procurator Pilate, the crowds yelling, "Crucify
Him!", the long dusty road to Calvary, the rough wooden
cross on which He died. It all seemed painfully unreal to the
disciples.

But Jesus' crucifixion and death were real. They lifted
His bloody, broken body from the cross. His followers
helped the women wrap His corpse in linen burial clothes.
They saw His shrouded form carried into that borrowed
tomb and sealed away forever. Now, fearing for their own
lives, the disciples hid together in a tiny room in Jerusalem,
trying to piece it all together.

Days passed. For seventy-two awful, lonely hours they
lived with their memories of that awful murder of their Master. Then on the evening of the third day, the women came
running to report that Jesus was risen from the dead. They
had seen Him and heard His voice. The disciples refused to
believe the evidence of an empty tomb and the piles of
empty graveclothes. Then two of Jesus' friends saw Him on
the road and ran to report His resurrection to the others.
The disciples still refused to believe these and other sight-
ings of their risen Lord. Finally, as the eleven sat down to
supper, He appeared to them and said:

Go ye into all the world, and preach the gospel to
every creature. He that believeth and is baptized
[washed] shall be saved; but he that believeth not shall
be damned.

Mark 16:15, 16 KJV

Then, reports eyewitness Mark, He left them and "was received up into heaven, and sat on the right hand of God" (v. 19 KJV).

The events of the next few weeks were as unbelievably wonderful as the crucifixion and burial of Jesus had been unbelievably bad. For days they prayed in their hideaway room as He had instructed them. For days they waited for the Spirit of God to come as He had promised. "I will not leave you comfortless," He told them. "When the Spirit is come, God the Father will give you another Comforter who will live with you forever and He will guide you into all truth" (*see* John 14:18, 26; 15:26).

As Jerusalem celebrated the feast of Pentecost, fifty days after His death and resurrection, the Spirit of God came unto the disciples in wind and fire. They ran into the streets, transformed by this new power in their lives. When Jews from around the world heard this noisy crowd of uneducated peasants testifying to the resurrection of Jesus, they were convicted and convinced—asking in many different languages, "What must we do to be saved?"

> Peter said to them:
> "Turn away from your sins [repent] . . . and be baptized [washed] in the name of Jesus Christ, so that your sins will be forgiven; and you will receive God's gift, the Holy Spirit."
>
> Acts 2:38 TEV

Wherever the disciples preached this good news, people repented and were baptized. Saul was converted and added to the list of apostles. Renamed Paul, his missionary journeys brought Christ's Gospel to the Gentiles (non-Jews). He preached in Corinth (Greece) and people believed. A new young church was born.

You may wonder how sexual lust fits into all of this. Now we've come back full cycle to where we began this chapter. It was that new young church in Corinth which received Paul's letter warning that adulterers, homosexuals, and fornicators could not possess or be included in this new Kingdom of God, except those who were washed, sanctified, and justified in the name of Jesus and in the Spirit of God.

Three Words of Truth

Now let's take a look at these three ancient words: *washed, sanctified,* and *justified.* Because, for all of us who struggle with temptation, for all of us who wonder what will happen if and when we lose the struggle with sexual lust, these three words represent the only truth in the world that can set us free from fear and give us courage to struggle on through success or failure.

We were washed.   To be washed means to be baptized. The Corinthian readers of Paul's ancient letter remembered that day when the apostle first taught them about Christian baptism. Paul waded into the sea with a young convert named Crispus, a leader of the synagogue in Corinth. His family stood on the nearby beach with a cluster of Christian believers. Paul prayed for Crispus, then took the young man in his arms and said for all to hear, "I baptize you in the name of Jesus Christ." The crowd on the shore knelt in the sand and sang an ancient hymn of praise. Tears streamed down the cheeks of family and friends as

Paul baptized Crispus in the sea.

Paul was teaching them that the ancient sacrificial system had ended forever. Jesus met the requirements of the law for everyone with His own shed blood. He had rescued them from a cruel and endless cycle that left them slaves to guilt and victims of those who would have them struggle all their lives to make adequate payment for their sin. No longer could unethical priests or clergymen force poor sinners to pay their way into the Kingdom of God. Jesus picked up the check for their sins and paid for their guilt forever. All He asked was that they believe and be baptized.

Two thousand years have passed since those first Christian baptisms. You may wonder why we moderns practice such an ancient rite. It is true that our confession of guilt (repentance) and our baptism (ceremonial washing) have roots in ancient Israel. It is also true that baptism wasn't original with Jesus. Other religions and cultures also practiced the ceremonial washing.

Nevertheless, for two thousand years the Christian church has followed Christ's command to baptize and be baptized. The means of administering the rite have varied over the centuries, but the meaning and the meaningfulness of baptism have never changed. Ask anyone who has been baptized. My pastor baptized me in the San Lorenzo River in Santa Cruz, California. I will never forget that day or how good I felt as we knelt together on the riverbank and sang, "It Is Well With My Soul."

Were you baptized in the country-church baptismal tank, a river, the ocean, or the nave of a great cathedral? Were you baptized as a believing adult—or have you gone on to appropriate for yourself your baptism as an infant? Were you baptized with high-church pagaentry, low-church simplicity, or charismatic excitement? Nothing changes the inward meaning of this outward act. For its meaning was established by what Christ did two thousand years ago.

Baptism is that moment when we publicly acknowledge His gift and say to all the world, "The guilt I carried for my sins was washed away forever by Christ's shed blood on the cross. He took my guilt away. He made me clean again."

Remember Shakespeare's tragedy of *Macbeth?* After the foul murder of the king, Lady Macbeth struggled helplessly with her growing feelings of guilt. Even after washing the blood away, she imagined bloodstains on her hands that would not come clean. Guilt pursued her and drove her mad. She wandered through the palace, rubbing at the imagined stains and crying, "Out, out, damned spot." Nothing she could do could make her feel clean again.

How is modern man or woman any different? Unrelieved guilt is filling up our hospitals and mental institutions. Unforgiving guilt makes alcoholics and drug addicts. Unhealthly guilt ruins marriages, friendships, churches, and communities.

So, when modern listeners cry out as did the crowds in Jerusalem after Peter's sermon at Pentecost, "What must we do to be saved?" the answer is today as it was then: "Repent [confess, feel regret, plead guilty, tell God you are sorry] and be baptized [tell the world that He has washed away your guilt forever]."

By now I hope it is getting clearer what the rite of baptism and the meaning of the rite have to do with those of us who struggle with sexual lust. Think of it! Our past sin is washed away. We don't have to carry that guilt baggage anymore. Through Christ we have a clean start. Through Him we can begin again.

We were sanctified. We can breathe a sigh of relief that our past guilt is washed away. But what about the present? How are we going to keep from giving in to sexual lust again and again? That's what this next long, theological word is all about. Like milk that stands on the dairy-counter shelf in a carton marked HOMOGENIZED, the Christian wears a label: SANCTIFIED. What does it mean? How does it help in our struggle against temptation?

The person who has repented and been baptized may feel no great difference in his life, but he or she is different, nevertheless, for that person has been invaded. *God's Spirit has moved into his or her life.* And His presence in us has all kinds of hopeful, helpful implications for our ongoing struggle with sexual lust.

Remember *The Miracle Worker,* that moving, true story of Helen Keller—blind, deaf, and dumb after an early-childhood disease and isolated in her dark and silent world? One day Miss Anne Sullivan moved into her life. The child Helen Keller could not know then that the love and patience and wisdom of her new teacher could change her from an "animal" into one of history's great human beings, but that is the difference which Anne Sullivan made when she came into Helen Keller's life.

This is what the Holy Spirit does for you and me. He moves into our lives, unpacks, and stays forever. He has come to release us from our slavery to animal passions and transforms us into sons and daughters of God. It will take our lifetimes. It will mean conflict and tension and hard decisions. But He is there to comfort us along the way. He encourages and loves us when we grow weary or afraid. He disciplines us when we get lazy or forgetful. He forgives us when we fail. He helps us change our values and rearrange our priorities. He is our Counselor, our Friend, our

Teacher, our Guide. He brings us joy.

On Christmas Eve, 1958, my hometown was inundated by a ten-foot wall of flood water. The next morning we all began to shovel mud out of homes and businesses. We waded through slimy, sticky goo to rescue family treasures. We washed down walls and removed debris. We took ruined homes and restored them. That is like the Holy Spirit, moving into the muck and ruin of our lives to restore, refurbish, rebuild, and redirect us.

So you struggle with sexual lust. Remember, you do not struggle alone. The Holy Spirit is in your life. Tell Him everything. Ask Him any questions. Let Him know how you feel or what you need or why you're angry or afraid. Open God's Word and let Him teach you through it. Be with Christian friends. Let Him speak to you through them. Let the first and last thought and first and last word of every day be focused on Him. He is for real. Take advantage of His presence in your life.

I can't believe how many of my fellow strugglers have never been turned on to the presence of the Holy Spirit. They believe He is there, but they don't experience Him. Prayer seems a dull, dry ritual, reading the Bible a chore. Let the Spirit change all that.

When I pray or read the Word or go to films and plays or run the beach or struggle with temptation, I talk to Him. "Hey, Spirit of God, are You here? Of course You are. Jesus promised You would be. What do You have for me today? Make me alive to what You are doing in the world. Awaken me to the changes You dream for my life. Forgive my failure. Thanks for my success."

That kind of daily running dialogue with the Holy Spirit can make a difference in your life, as it has in mine. When sexual lust begins its dance of death, talk long and hard to Him:

Spirit of God, I am tempted now. Don't let me forget Your long-range dreams for my life. Don't let me trade them in for some short-term sexual thrill. Keep me safe, Lord, from the evil working on me this moment. Protect me. Make me strong. Guide me. I love You, Lord; I am Yours. I want Your will more than anything. I will not throw that away.

Prayer is not just talking to ourselves. Dialogue with the Holy Spirit is not just a meditation technique to help quiet our souls and clarify our direction. When we pray, we are talking to the Living God. He is really present with us. The Holy Spirit is a living, moving, acting power inside our lives, waiting for our permission to do His work in and through us. You are sanctified. The Spirit of God is in you. Let Him be the faithful, loving, powerful Ally whom God promises you in your struggle with carnal temptation.

We were justified. Does all that mean the Holy Spirit will mysteriously transport us out of temptation's battle zone, as the *Star Trek* crew were transported out of harm's way through the magic of the spaceship *Enterprise?* Does the Holy Spirit remove the source of our temptations, as Disney characters disappear in a puff of animated dust? Will we never fail again when tempted by sexual lust—because the Holy Spirit swoops down like Superman and lifts us safely away?

No. Though God's Spirit lives and works in each of us, the spirit of the Evil One still has some power in our lives. We live in two worlds simultaneously. Through the Holy Spirit, God's new age is dawning in our lives, but the long night of evil has not yet ended. From time to time we will lose the battle between good and evil in our lives. There is the real possibility that we will fail in our struggle against sexual lust.

If so, you must be asking, "Aren't we back to where this chapter began? If we fail in our struggle with sexual lust, then we must be adulterers or homosexuals or fornicators. And if, as Paul warned, adulterers, homosexuals, and fornicators cannot possess the Kingdom of God, then we are in bad trouble."

Don't panic. Here's where justification makes all the difference. Paul proclaims the good news this way: "Although all have sinned and come short of the glory of God, we are justified [declared free of blame, absolved of guilt, forgiven] through the act of liberation in the person of Jesus Christ" (*see* Romans 3:23, 24).

"But," you say, "we already went through that when we discussed baptism. We already agreed that Christ's death on the cross paid—once and for all—the penalty of our *past* guilt. But what about our present and future failures? Do they drag us back to 'square one' all over again? Are we *safe,* then *out* again? Is every lost battle a lost war?"

No! Justification means that what Christ did to save us from past guilt saves us from future guilt as well. Paul describes it this way: "And so, since we have now been justified [declared free of blame, absolved of guilt, forgiven] by Christ's sacrificial death, we shall all the more certainly be saved through him from final retribution" (Romans 5:9). Again he writes:

If on your lips is the confession, "Jesus is Lord," and in your heart the faith that God raised him from the dead, then you will find salvation. For the faith that leads to righteousness [declared free of blame, absolved of guilt, forgiven] is in the heart . . . .

Romans 10:9, 10

For it is by his grace you are saved [declared free of blame, absolved of guilt, forgiven], through trusting him; it is not your own doing. It is God's gift, not a reward for work done.

Ephesians 2:8, 9

I wish I had known about "justification" when I was a teenage struggler. No one taught me about God's free grace in those days. I tried so hard to be good. I tried so hard to conquer my sexual feelings. Every time I failed, I thought I had lost my salvation for sure.

On the front page of the *Los Angeles Times* in April 1976, there was a sad picture of grieving parents at the burial rites of their son. The reporter told the tragic tale of this young man, who hanged himself in jail after his mistaken arrest for a charge that had already been dropped from the books.

We don't need to live in fear anymore. We have been justified. The charges against us have been dropped forever. Jesus paid the penalty for us on the cross, two thousand years ago.

Of course, justification doesn't mean that you can quit struggling against temptation. It means we go on struggling. It means we yield ourselves as completely as we can to the influence of the Holy Spirit in our lives. It means we work as hard as we can never to become lazy or careless. It means we still ask His and each other's forgiveness when we fail. Remember, I have already discussed the ongoing struggle and our responsibility to do our best. Now it's time to celebrate. So many people are afraid we'll go off the deep end that few really celebrate God's grace or more than whisper about His free gift of justification. We should take to the streets with marching bands and banners reading:

CELEBRATE! WE'VE BEEN PARDONED. Luther's words would be perfect for a Latin bumper sticker: SEMPER JUSTUS, SEMPER PECCATOR. In my rough translation that means, God sees us as justified, absolved of guilt, forgiven—even though we still see ourselves as sinners.

When Paul wrote our text: "Make no mistake, no fornicator, no homosexual, no adulterer will possess the kingdom of God," he wrote with a gleam in his eye and a shout of joy on his lips. We have been washed, sanctified, and *justified* (in spite of our failures along the way). We are adulterers, homosexuals, fornicators no more.

We began this chapter asking, "Will we ever win the struggle with sexual lust?" Paul is trying to tell us that He has already won it for us. The apostle was shouting the good news that, though we may lose battles on the way, Christ has already won the war. There may be no miraculous escape from temptation, but the miracle of the cross removes forever the penalty of our sins—past, present, and even in the future.

Don't believe those who offer easy, permanent miraculous cures for your struggle with sexual lust. No one can say, "Follow my diet and you will never be fat again." Neither can anyone say, "Christians who are washed, sanctified, and justified will never struggle with sexual lust again."

But take heart. You will see victories along the way. And—because you have been washed, sanctified, and justified—even when you lose, you win. Even when you fail, God sees you as a winner. That is the mystery of the Carpenter from Nazareth, His bloody death on a Roman cross, and the empty tomb. Something Jesus did on the cross that day put us in God's victory circle even when we lose the race. Celebrate, fellow strugglers, God's amazing grace!

SUMMARY

Story 7: Jesus, the Cross, and the Empty Tomb
(Will I Ever Win the Struggle With Sexual Lust?)

A book like this should end with "Ten Perfect Steps That You Can Follow to Win Your Struggle With Sexual Lust." Sorry, folks. It isn't so. You will see victories along the way, but still from time to time you will fail.

The good news is this: Whether you see yourself as a winner or as a loser, God sees you as a winner. That is the mystery at the heart of this chapter—the mystery of the Carpenter from Nazareth, His bloody death on a Roman cross and His miraculous resurrection from the dead. Something He did on the cross two thousand years ago puts us in the victory circle even when we lose the race. Celebrate, fellow strugglers with *all* kinds of temptation, God's amazing grace!

Matthew 26–28 Mark 14–16 Luke 22–24 John 13–21	The Story of the Cross and the Empty Tomb.
Acts 2:14–40	Peter's sermon on the meaning of the cross and the empty tomb and his advice: 1. Repent. 2. Be baptized in Jesus' name for the forgiveness of sins. 3. And you shall receive the gift of the Holy Spirit.

1 Corinthians 6:9–11   Paul's good news about what
                        the cross and empty tomb
                        could do for those who strug-
                        gle with sexual lust:
                        1. Jesus took care of the past:
                           "You are washed."
                        2. Jesus took care of the
                           present: "You are sanc-
                           tified."
                        3. Jesus took care of the fu-
                           ture: "You are justified."

Story 8

JESUS AND HIS PEOPLE
(Must I Struggle Alone?)

I will never forget the day I first confessed my problems with sexual temptation to another human being. For too long I had worried and wondered and felt guilty alone. During that time I had confessed my struggle with sexual lust to God in private prayers and in public worship, but I had never talked about it to another person.

Finally I made an appointment to see a Fuller Seminary school psychologist. I knew I had to tell someone, since I couldn't seem to solve the problems by myself; so I chose a safe, professional listener. Even that step wasn't easy. Calling the Counseling Center to make an appointment was nerve-wracking. Sitting in the counselors' waiting room and watching my fellow students come and go made me feel embarrassed. Entering Dr. Don Tweedie's office and hearing him say, "How can I help you?" left me tongue-tied and stammering.

I had never gone to a psychologist before. I was struggling against all the prejudices I carried about professional counseling—and all the fear I had about being exposed. I still didn't realize that my problems were neither different from nor more serious than anybody else's. I couldn't know then that sharing my problems would end the cycle of secrecy and begin a process of healing. In spite of all my fears (and because the hour was costing me twenty-five hard-earned dollars), I blurted out the whole story of my sexual lust.

I don't know what I expected the psychologist's reaction to be, but when I had finished, he smiled and asked me, "Have you told your wife?"

"Of course not," I replied, dumbfounded.

"Well, you had better," he said. Then he stood to signal that my time was up. I almost died of shock and apprehension.

I thought psychologists were supposed to nod pleasantly, smile supportingly, and listen silently. Instead Dr. Tweedie nodded, smiled, listened, then dropped the bomb. He warned me against keeping secrets from my wife and led me to the door. I could barely share my sexual lust with a professional psychologist who heard stories like mine every day of his life and whom I would never have to see again. How could I tell my wife—with whom I planned to spend the rest of my life?

For three awful weeks I tried to tell her—and for two more weeks I made excuses and failed miserably. Finally I decided his advice was right enough to risk my pride.

I picked up my wife at Crescenta Valley High School where she taught literature. I took her out to a surprise dinner in a quiet little restaurant with dark, private booths.

I could hardly swallow a bite of food. Small talk wasn't working. I dropped my fork and, picking it up again, I bumped my head on the table. I laughed nervously. I thought I was coming unglued. The evening almost ended in a comedy of errors, with my secrets still hidden from the person I loved most. Just before dessert I finally got up my courage and told her everything—at least enough to make it clear that though I loved her and though our sex life scored "good" to "great," I still had struggles.

Bonhoeffer on Confession

I have learned a lot about confession since that first feeble attempt—from my wife, from an expanding circle of people to whom I confess regularly, and from Dietrich Bonhoeffer's little book *Life Together*. His biblical and theological insights into the role of confession in the Christian community, as well as my own personal experiences of confession, have convinced me of the great importance of confession in our struggle with temptation.

You probably already know the life and writings of Dietrich Bonhoeffer, the young German pastor who risked his life to keep the church in Germany from giving in to Hitler's tyranny. In 1935 the anti-Nazi Confessional Church called Pastor Bonhoeffer to take charge of their illegal underground seminary in Pomerania. For three years, he and approximately twenty-five theological students and pastors lived, studied, worked, and played together in an old estate house in Finkendwalde.

Out of their shared experiences in Christian community, Bonhoeffer wrote *Life Together*. All the quotations that follow are from the last short chapter of his profoundly simple work. In 1938 the underground seminary that produced the community which Bonhoeffer describes was closed by the Gestapo. After two years of imprisonment, on April 9, 1945, Pastor Bonhoeffer was executed by the Nazis just days before their defeat by the Allies.

The kind of personal confession of sin by one person to another that Bonhoeffer and his students practiced has been largely neglected, in my experience of evangelical Christianity. I remember visiting a European cathedral and seeing the wooden stalls and iron gates and thick curtains of the old Catholic confessionals. I remember how awful it all sounded to me then and how glad and proud I was that we

Protestants could "go directly to God when we prayed." I remember my elementary-school Catholic classmates laughing about telling the same old story in confession in order to get their weekly treat from parent or priest. I never did get past my prejudices to see the positive side of confession, Catholic or otherwise.

So I wrote off confession because of the criticisms (real or imagined) that I had heard. In its place we young evangelicals were encouraged to confess our sinfulness (in general terms) at conversion, but thereafter we had no regular, systematic way to confess the specific sins that followed. As a result, confession was made to God in secret (if it were made at all) and seldom if ever did we confess to a brother or sister in Christ.

We forget that confession to each other was practiced during Bible times: "And Saul said unto Samuel, I have sinned . . ." (1 Samuel 15:24 KJV)—"And David said unto Nathan, I have sinned against the Lord . . ." (2 Samuel 12:13 KJV)—And Paul wrote to Timothy: "Christ came to save sinners, of whom I am chief" (*see* 1 Timothy 1:15). Bonhoeffer reminds us of the Apostle James's New Testament command: "Confess your faults one to another, and pray one for another, that ye may be healed . . ." (James 5:16 KJV). Jesus said to His disciples, "Whose soever sins you forgive, they are forgiven unto them" (*see* John 20:23).

My experience of confession was quite the opposite. We always confessed to God in secret and rarely made confession to a brother or sister. Bonhoeffer may have been a German Lutheran pastor, but in *Life Together* he describes perfectly my experience growing up in an American evangelical church. He tells it like it was for me—why I didn't or couldn't confess my sins to anyone but God. He also describes the terrible loneliness I felt when no one knew or understood or could help me in my struggles.

He who is alone with his sin is utterly alone. It may be that Christians, notwithstanding corporate worship, common prayer, and all their fellowship in service, may still be left to their loneliness. The final break-through to fellowship does not occur, because, though they have fellowship with one another as believers and as devout people, they do not have fellowship as the undevout, as sinners. The pious fellowship permits no one to be a sinner. So everybody must conceal his sin from himself and from the fellowship. We dare not be sinners. Many Christians are unthinkably horrified when a real sinner is suddenly discovered among the righteous. So we remain alone with our sin, living in lies and hypocrisy. The fact is that we *are* sinners!

We could get bogged down here in theological word games. Some of our brothers and sisters correct Bonhoeffer and say, "We are not sinners." Others of us use euphemistic language to describe our "faults" or "errors" or "mistakes" and don't like to say that Christians do sin. Others of us proclaim almost too loudly, "We are sinners still." However you want to describe life after conversion, every Christian I know intimately struggles with various temptations and occasionally fails in that struggle. Bonhoeffer suggests that person-to-person confession is a great and God-given aid to help us in those times of failure.

Don't worry. Pastor Bonhoeffer is not suggesting that we should confess to each other *instead* of to God. Nor is he saying we can forgive each other apart from Christ's work on the cross. But he does wonder why you and I find it so easy to confess to God (who is a holy and sinless foe of disobedience)—yet we find it difficult to confess to our brothers and sisters (who sin as we sin).

Confession Is a Breakthrough to God

Bonhoeffer suggests that perhaps all along we have been confessing our sins to ourselves and not to God. Perhaps this is the reason "for our countless relapses and the feebleness of our Christian obedience." He says that real forgiveness, God's forgiveness, can come best through confession to our brothers and sisters. They can break the "cycle of self-deception." They can bring "to the light" the full reality of what we are doing. And Bonhoeffer adds, "But since the sin must come to light some time, it is better that it happens today between me and my brother, rather than on the last day in the piercing light of the final judgment."

That is exactly what happened when I confessed my sin to the Christian psychologist. After confessing many times to God, it took one confession to a brother to help me hear God's voice and to realize the long-range harm this secretiveness could be to my marriage. After an hour I learned from a Christian brother the immediate and lifetime help my wife could be if she, too, shared my struggle. God did not get that through my thick skull until I heard Him through my confession to a fellow believer.

When I confessed to Lyla, I learned in a brand-new way about God's judgment and God's grace. Bonhoeffer says it this way: "As the open confession of my sins to a brother insures me against self-deception, so, too, the assurance of forgiveness becomes fully certain when it is spoken by a brother in the name of God."

Sometimes I think I kept my struggle a secret so long in order to enjoy my sexual lust when and if I desired it. Now that Lyla knows, all of that has changed. Now it is not so easy to lust as it was before. I judge my actions through her eyes. I see my behavior as she sees it. I make decisions in dialogue with her, and she confronts me with hard questions when I need to be confronted. And she shows her disappointment, her grief, and her anger when I make the wrong decision in spite of knowing better.

Before I confessed to my wife, I knew that God was present at the site of my struggle with sexual lust, but it didn't make half the difference that it makes to know that Lyla is present, too. Isn't that crazy? Suddenly *she* is teaching me how seriously God views my sin. I see Him watching me in her eyes. Because my confession brought her into the ongoing process, she is teaching me about God's judgment.

But she also taught me about God's grace. In spite of my lust, she loved and forgave me. She is far from "saintly." She is as human as anyone, but her love has come through for me in spite of my struggle. I see God's love in her eyes as I never saw it when I confessed to Him in secret.

Confession Is a Breakthrough to Community

We American evangelicals have a reputation for our independence and our individuality. Like our little children we say, "I can do it myself." We don't really believe we need each other. Bonhoeffer disagreed. He didn't think we could survive apart from authentic Christian community and he believed that confession—one to another—can result in our breakthrough into Christian community. He says it this way in *Life Together:*

> In confession the break-through to [Christian] community takes place. Sin demands to have a man by himself. It withdraws him from the community. The more isolated a person is, the more destructive will be the power of sin over him, and the more deeply he

becomes involved in it, the more disastrous is his isolation.

All those years I spent in isolation, I was a member of the Christian church. But until I confessed my secret struggles, I didn't really understand the meaning of authentic Christian community. There are now more than a dozen Christian brothers and sisters who know me intimately. Along with everything else, I have confessed my struggle with sexual lust to them. As a result I am discovering the following about the Christian community . . . .

The community can be trusted.   We live in fear that someone will hear our secrets and tell them to the world. And because we are afraid of being exposed, we isolate ourselves and hide our sins. We cut off ourselves and our struggles from community. It is better to take the risk of being exposed than to take the risk of secrecy. Secret sins are, as Bonhoeffer promised, deadly sins. Besides, I am confident, after a ten-year test, that our brothers and sisters can be trusted.

You may have had a different experience. Almost universally I am told, "You can't trust anybody, especially Christians." And I , too, have seen rumors passed on as prayer requests or church announcements. But have we really been so badly betrayed as we claim? Or is it just another excuse to keep our sins secret? Could your fear of betrayal be one more rationalization keeping you from the joy of real community?

Lyla and I have been in different study and discussion groups for more than a dozen years. Hardly a week goes by that we haven't met with someone to talk and eat, study and pray. Although some of the groups have been more sharing than others, all have been intimate in some degree. Yet not once in twelve years have our secrets been revealed. None of that talk—and there were millions of words dropped on carpets and coffee tables—has ever come back to haunt us. I believe the Christian community can be trusted.

The community can help us. Ask a person why he or she has never confessed his or her struggle with sexual lust to the Christian community, and you will probably get one of the following answers: "Even if I could trust them, no one I know would really understand." Or "Are you kidding? No one in my community is qualified to deal with my problem." Or "If church people knew about my secrets, they would kick me out." Or "I don't want to hurt anybody else's faith or lead him into temptation."

We don't believe the community could handle our problems, because we think that our problems are unique. It isn't true. In fact, it is a dangerous and misleading self-deception to believe that our sexual lust is so different from everybody else's. Our struggles may be unique to us, but we are not the first or only person to deal with similar struggles, whatever they are, not even in our church. We do not sin more wickedly or suffer more deeply than everybody else. And we do not have to go on alone with our secret struggle. The community can help us.

Admittedly, we don't confess to everyone. There are only a few people in the world who know everything about my various temptations. The ultimate details of my struggles are not the world's business, any more than your intimate struggles are your entire church's business.

You may not choose to confess to your husband or wife first. You may not decide to confess to him or her at all. Perhaps a friend would be a better place to start. In the process, ask that friend how he or she feels about your

confessing to your husband or wife. Trust God to lead you
through that friend. Maybe you want to confess first to a
Christian stranger.

I started on the road to confession with a professional
Christian counselor whom I had never met before. It was a
safe and more comfortable way to begin. I will always be
grateful for the services of the professional counseling
community. However, we must not underestimate the help-
fulness of our untrained brothers and sisters in Christ.
Bonhoeffer wrote in *Life Together:* "In the presence of a
psychiatrist I can only be a sick man; in the presence of a
Christian brother I can dare to be a sinner." Forty years
ago he wrote these prophetic words:

> Worldly wisdom knows what distress and weakness
> and failure are, but it does not know the godlessness of
> man. And so it also does not know that man is de-
> stroyed only by his sin and can be healed only by for-
> giveness . . . . Anybody . . . who has discerned in
> the Cross of Jesus the utter wickedness of all men and
> of his own heart will find there is no sin that can ever be
> alien to him . . . .
>
> It is not experience of life but experience of the
> Cross that makes one a worthy hearer of confes-
> sions . . . . The Christian brother knows when I
> come to him: here is a sinner like myself, a godless man
> who wants to confess and yearns for God's forgive-
> ness . . . . The brother views me as I am before the
> judging and merciful God in the Cross of Jesus Christ.
> It is not lack of psychological knowledge but lack of
> love for the crucified Jesus Christ that makes us so
> poor and inefficient in brotherly confession.

We may not be able to help each other as long-range
therapists. In fact, we may want to suggest in the face of

serious symptoms that professional help be sought immediately. But anyone who has admitted and confessed his or her own sinfulness to God should be able to accept and then love and forgive and pray for someone else whose confession we hear without shock or judgment or fear.

I have taken graduate courses in psychology. I have been trained as a pastor-therapist. I have been around the professional psychological community for two decades. But I am still not qualified to understand my need for God's forgiveness. Because others have forgiven me in the name of Christ, I can hear another person's confession. I can pray with him and accept him without feeling superior or shocked or surprised. I can demonstrate God's judgment (by confronting sin when necessary) and I can demonstrate God's grace (by loving the sinner always). I am not a therapist—but I am a Christian brother. I do not offer long-term treatment—but I do offer forgiveness in the name of Christ. You can offer that to others, and your Christian community can offer that to you.

What Is Confession?

Confession is *not* a technique for building community or for developing closeness among Christian brothers and sisters. Sensitivity groups, encounter games, and relational leaders have a significant place in the church, since church people, like everyone else, need to express themselves more freely. Christians, too, need times to "let it all hang out." But manipulated intimacy can lead to disappointment and tragedy.

How many times I have seen a brother or sister persuaded to attend an encounter seminar or small-group weekend. Suddenly he finds himself in a circle of smiling, accepting, encouraging, loving faces. Before he (or she) knows it, he has taken the risk. He has stripped off his mask. He has taken their advice to tell all. Then, just as suddenly, the seminar ends and the weekend is over. All the smiling, accepting, encouraging, loving faces have disappeared. Even that warm, charismatic leader is gone on to the next weekend seminar. The brother or sister is alone again. There is no one left who really cares and one feels tricked and betrayed. Confession can be a dangerous technique for building community.

Confession should not be a means of getting sympathy and support, either. It is exciting to tell a close friend your struggles with sexual lust. And even better if he or she confesses back to you. It is like telling ghost stories around the campfire. Shared fear draws the circle closer. People huddle together, haunted by the same fears. One story leads to another. It's a kind of game and it isn't confession at all.

In fact, how many sexual affairs were started by someone confessing his or her sexual struggle—all the while using that confession to entice the very person who is hearing it? Though this may masquerade as confession, it is really just another clever technique to flirt or seduce or gain sympathy from a curious and vulnerable friend.

Confession cannot be a routine duty or obligation, either. Bonhoeffer says that "confession as a pious work is an invention of the devil." Maybe he is remembering the junior-high student who makes his weekly confession only because it pleases priest or parent. Maybe he is thinking about long-time members of the church who stand to recite (in unison) a confession of sin as a dull and thoughtless routine of worship. I wonder if he even knows about the person who goes down the sawdust trail or coliseum stairs to confess—just because it makes him acceptable to the busload of believers who brought him to the crusade.

Whomever Bonhoeffer is thinking about, he warns us all in *Life Together* of what confession should be:

> It is only God's offer of grace, help, and forgiveness that could make us dare to enter the abyss of confession. We can confess solely for the sake of the promise of absolution. Confession as a routine duty is spiritual death; confession in reliance upon the promise is life.

Then in one short sentence Bonhoeffer describes confession in words that have pursued and excited me: "The forgiveness of sins is the sole ground and goal of confession."

I didn't understand Bonhoeffer's sense of confession when I first told Lyla the details of my struggle with sexual lust. Passing information to another person, regardless of how intimate or secret that information might be, is not "confession" to Bonhoeffer. To him, confession is the act of seeking God's forgiveness in Christ through a Christian brother or sister.

What a difference that goal makes when we confess! We are not there to get sympathy (no matter how good that feels). We are not confessing to get another's counsel or advice (though that, too, might result from our confession). We are confessing to get our sins up out of the secret darkness (where we have hidden them) into God's pure light. We want forgiveness from Him for our sins. Our brothers or sisters do not replace God. They demonstrate God's judgment and mercy in their response and point us to Him, the only One who can forgive. As our brothers and sisters forgive us, they bring us the good news that He forgives us, too. Of course you can confess to God in secret. There is no law that anyone else need be involved. But what a help my brothers and sisters in Christ have been to me when I hear them say, "Because God forgives you, I forgive you, too." And what support they have been, in the days that follow, to keep me from having to make that same confession again.

SUMMARY

Story 8: Jesus and His People
(Must I Struggle Alone?)

One morning, just after Christ left them, His disciples were gathered in an upper room. Jesus was gone. They must have wondered how they could make it without Him. Suddenly the room rocked with wind and fire. God had come again to be with them in person (the Spirit) and in community (the church). To win the war with sexual lust is to stop struggling alone and to start taking advantage of His presence and His people.

The Spirit of God's first work was to build the body of Christ. Read about the first-century church and how they loved each other (Acts 2:41–47; 4:31–37).

At the heart of this chapter is a young German pastor, Dietrich Bonhoeffer, who loved Christ's church and gave his own life to save it from Hitler's Third Reich. His experiments in confession and Christian community in an illegal underground seminary are recorded in his little book *Life Together.* Bonhoeffer's experience got me started in a personal experiment in Christian confession that has revolutionized my ideas about body life in the church.

John 20:23	Jesus' Commission to Confession
James 5:16	The Apostle's Command to Confession
Life Together	Bonhoeffer's Experiments in Confession

Story 9

PAUL AND THE SCANDAL IN CORINTH
(What New Testament Guidelines Are There to Follow?)

Sex scandals are not new in the church. Almost two thousand years ago, incest was discovered in the mission at Corinth. It wasn't the scandal but the new believer's indifference to it that sent Paul, the church's founder, racing to write:

> I actually hear reports of sexual immorality among you, immorality such as even pagans do not tolerate: the union of a man with his father's wife. And you can still be proud of yourselves! You ought to have gone into mourning . . . this man is to be consigned to Satan for the destruction of the body, so that his spirit may be saved on the Day of the Lord.
>
> 1 Corinthians 5:1–5

Modern readers may wince at Paul's seemingly hysterical reaction to this case of sexual lust. In light of today's standards, Paul's penalty suggestions seem extremely harsh. Who can imagine what it would mean for our churches to "consign to Satan" or "root out of the church" one of our members caught in incest, adultery, or homosexuality? Apparently, Paul took sexual lust a lot more seriously than most Christians would today.

There were reasons for Paul's response. To understand them we must go back to Corinth. Paul had just planted this new young church in a notorious city famous for its vice and prostitution. The Corinthian temple to Aphrodite was serviced by a thousand prostitutes. Men, married or unmarried, could buy and sell women for sexual intercourse with no fear of censure by the public. In fact, a common Greek name for prostitute was translated "a Corinthian woman."

When the newly trained leaders of the young church faltered in the face of sexual immorality, Paul acted quickly. His harsh words to them were calculated to cause them pain and to wound their feelings, in order that they would "take the matter seriously" (*see* 2 Corinthians 7:8–11). At stake was more than the rescue of one guilty man and his victim. The future of the entire church was in jeopardy. In their indifference to sexual lust, the people had betrayed their indifference to the truth and their insensitivity to the leading of God's Holy Spirit. Instead of struggling to find God's way, the Corinthians had given in to the pagan standards of their neighbors. Unless Paul acted quickly and with force, sexual lust and the people's indifference toward it meant the beginning of the end for his children at Corinth.

There is no way to organize or systematize these two letters. Paul didn't write in tidy theological outlines. There is no way to distill Paul's pat formula for dealing with sexual lust in his rambling, emotional letters. But we can get a helpful look into Paul's heart as he struggled to teach his faltering church how they could win the struggle with sexual lust in their pagan, pleasure-seeking world.

Paul Saw Life As Warfare

To understand Paul's reaction to sexual lust we must understand how the apostle viewed life itself. For him, each person was a battlefield where God waged war with Satan for that person's soul. This view of life as warfare permeates all the letters of Paul to his mission congregations throughout the world.

To the church in Philippi, he wrote: ". . . work out your own salvation in fear and trembling" (Philippians 2:12). To his beloved disciple Timothy, Paul wrote: "So fight gallantly, armed with faith and a good conscience . . ." (1 Timothy 1:19) and "Take your share of hardship, like a good soldier of Christ Jesus" (2 Timothy 2:3). To the new Christians at Colossae the apostle wrote: "Be on your guard; do not let your minds be captured . . ." (Colossians 2:8). Paul confessed his own spiritual warfare to the Christians at Rome:

> . . . when I want to do the right, only the wrong is within my reach. In my inmost self I delight in the law of God, but I perceive that there is in my bodily members a different law, fighting against the law that my reason approves and making me a prisoner . . . .
>
> Romans 7:21–24

To his friends at Thessalonica, Paul wrote: "Stand firm, then, brothers, and hold fast . . ." (2 Thessalonians 2:15).

Paul was not just a tight-lipped Puritan with skirts gathered around him, his finger pointed in judgment at the guilty man in Corinth. Paul acted harshly so that the guilty person's spirit might be "saved on the day of the Lord Jesus" (*see* 1 Corinthians 5:5). The apostle explained in his follow-up letter why he had been so strict with the faltering believers in the mission church: "For Satan must not be allowed to get the better of us . . ." (2 Corinthians 2:11).

Paul took sexual lust seriously because he saw it as one of Satan's many tricks to win his way into the life of the Christian believer and eventually crowd out and defeat the influence of the Holy Spirit. Sexual lust was one more tactic used by the Evil One to win the war for man's soul.

Christ Has Won the War

Now the irony of Paul's position becomes apparent. The apostle knew that throughout history people had experienced and described in various ways this war between good and evil in human life. He knew, too, that different solutions had been suggested from the beginning of time. To Paul, until his conversion to Christ, no solution had really proven adequate. "Jews call for miracles," Paul reminded the Corinthians, "Greeks look for wisdom; but we proclaim Christ—yes, Christ nailed to the cross . . ." (1 Corinthians 1:23).

Paul knew that to suggest that Jesus' death on a cross was a final victory over evil in the war for people's souls would be a "stumbling block" to Jews and "folly" to the Greeks. Nevertheless, right from the beginning of his correspondence to them, Paul reaffirmed the basic Christian solution to this age-old war. "This doctrine of the cross is sheer folly to those on their way to ruin," he warned them, "but to us who are on the way to salvation it is the power of God" (1 Corinthians 1:18).

Not only is the war ended for the Christian believer, but God gives power to guarantee the victory. ". . . he is our righteousness," Paul affirmed; "in him we are consecrated and set free" (1 Corinthians 1:30). So, at the outset, Paul declared that the war between good and evil had been won. Christ had won it for them on the cross.

But the Battles Go On

Then the irony continued. Though Christ had won the war for all people and all times, Paul warned them that the battle was not over yet. Though he promised them that "[God] will keep you firm to the end, without reproach on the Day of our Lord Jesus" (1 Corinthians 1:8), they must go on fighting. There would be tests and temptations. Satan would do his best to destroy the work that God was doing in them. The war had been won, but the battles continued.

Paul himself felt the dilemma. He confessed to the Corinthians his own ". . . fear that after preaching to others I should find myself rejected" (1 Corinthians 9:27). Later in the same letter he boldly affirmed the opposite: "God keeps faith, and he will not allow you to be tested above your powers, but when the test comes he will at the same time provide a way out, by enabling you to sustain it" (10:13).

Paul lived on the sharp edge of both realities. He knew God had won the war for him in Christ and yet he also knew well the struggle between good and evil that went on in him. So he didn't try to save the Corinthians from the warfare that he felt. Instead he encouraged them to live in healthy tension between confidence in what Christ had done (and would do) for them to win the war and the hard, painful, and risky decisions they must make in the battles that would continue.

Apparently, the new Christians in Corinth were overconfident about what Christ had done. They had been "washed, sanctified, and justified in Christ," as Paul reminded them. And in Christ they had been freed from the deadly restrictions of Old Testament Law. As a result, the believers felt (as one said): "I am free to do anything." Sexual lust and the church's lenience towards the guilty party came as a result of this one-sided view of Christian warfare. They had been born again, but they didn't understand that new birth was the beginning and not the end of the struggle in their lives.

The Body Is a Battlefield

The Corinthians had been sold another one-sided view about their physical bodies by Greek thinkers and their "Hollywood T-shirt" ideas. "The body is only a house," the pagan philosophers reasoned, "a temporary home for your spirit. Don't take it too seriously. It's just a machine to maintain and amuse you. Discipline your spirit, but let your body do its thing."

". . . but it is not true that the body is for lust," Paul answered them; "it is for the Lord . . . ." In his letter he described three significant facts about a Christian's body: (1) "Your body is a shrine of the indwelling Holy Spirit"; (2) "Your bodies are the limbs and organs of Christ"; (3) "God not only raised our Lord from the dead; he will also raise us by his power" (*see* 1 Corinthians 6:13–19).

The Christian religion wasn't something that happened only in their heads, Paul explained. God's Spirit had invaded their bodies. (They had a new power.) Their bodies became Christ's body. (They had a new purpose.) Their bodies would be given life eternal. (They had a new future.) For believers in Corinth, where the human body was often only a toy for orgies of feasting and sexual intercourse, Paul's announcement must have surprised and startled them.

Picture them running to their full-length mirrors to stare at their bodies in this new light. Imagine them seeing their bald heads and bulging bellies as the temples where God lived—and their toga-draped limbs as the hands and feet of Jesus in the world. These dark-skinned, garlic-breathing believers saw themselves for the first time as God's "forever people" who will climb triumphant from the grave.

Guidelines to Help in the Battle

Corinth was a wide-open port city. People there could get sex any way they wanted it. Paul never implied that sexual intercourse was of itself evil. So, after his strong warnings against sexual lust, the new Corinthian Christians must have wondered which sex acts were "bad" and which were "good."

Paul's list of "illegal" sex acts is complete only to those without much imagination. It is clear that he condemns incest (sexual intercourse with your children or relatives other than your husband or wife), adultery (sexual intercourse with someone else's husband or wife), and sodomy (though translated as "homosexual perversion," it means literally either the passive or active partner in sexual intercourse between two males).

It is not clear that Paul condemns all other forms of sexual intercourse outside of marriage. Where our English translations read "fornication," Paul's original Greek word was *porneia,* which means "to sell" and refers to slaves bought and sold for prostitution. Where Paul was condemning prostitution or trafficking in slaves for that purpose, the Latin fathers substituted *fornicatio,* which led readers to believe that Paul was condemning all forms of premarital sexual intercourse.

We do, however, have two clues that Paul believed that sexual intercourse was appropriate *only* for marriage partners. In his solution for those who cannot control their sexual desires, Paul said, ". . . they should marry. Better be married than burn with vain desire" (1 Corinthians 7:9).

Second, since Paul was a follower of Jesus, he certainly remembered the Master's words: ". . . If a man looks on a woman with a lustful eye [sexual intercourse on his mind],

he has already committed adultery with her in his heart"
(Matthew 5:28).

Even then Jesus was trying to teach His followers about
responsible freedom. They wanted Him to tell them what
was right and what was wrong. They wanted new laws to
replace the Old Testament Law. "How far can we go without sinning?" was the wrong question to ask Jesus (or
Paul). They both were preparing God's new people for
God's new freedom in the Spirit. The old law was dead.
They wanted the believers to let God's living Word lead
them to exciting new levels of purity in mind and body and
as far away as possible from thoughts or actions that dehumanize and enslave.

Paul wasn't about to add his list to the Old Testament
Law of Moses. In fact, he compared and contrasted the
Jews' bondage to the old law with the believers' new free-
dom in Christ. Paul wrote: "The written law condemns to
death" (*see* 2 Corinthians 3:6), but "where the Spirit of the
Lord is, there is liberty" (*see* v. 17).

Like Jesus, Paul was teaching the new believers how to
handle freedom responsibly. To this end he advised them:
". . . each one must order his life according to the gift the
Lord has granted him and his condition when God called
him" (1 Corinthians 7:17).

Thus the Corinthian Christians—who wanted Paul to tell
them what they could and could not do sexually—must
have felt terribly frustrated by the apostle's limited sexual-
lust list. His general advice—"Glorify God in your body"
(*see* 1 Corinthians 6:20 KJV)—must have left the believers
wondering how they would ever be sure what was right and
what was wrong. The old law was no longer an adequate
standard. And the believers' new freedom in Christ demanded that they make many decisions for themselves

about what was good or bad. There were still guidelines to help them—in the Old Testament, in the life and words of Jesus, and the teaching of the apostles (the developing New Testament).

Let the Holy Spirit Help You in Your Battle

It is possible that when the believers in Corinth finished reading Paul's first letter, one complained, "Christian freedom is difficult. If we are supposed to make decisions for ourselves about what is good and bad, then give me the Ten Commandments any day. At least with the Law of Moses we knew what we were doing wrong." And that is all the old law could do, as Paul warned them: "The written law condemns to death."

But when God first gave the law to Moses, Paul explained, ". . . it was inaugurated with divine splendour." He didn't mean for the Commandments ("Thou shalt not . . .") to just condemn the people, but to guide their relationships to Him and to each other. God was there with the law to guide and enable and forgive the people. But the people's minds became insensitive to the present though invisible God. Their unbelief veiled their eyes to Him (Problem Number One). All they had left were the cold, condemning laws they could not obey (Problem Number Two). (*See* 2 Corinthians 3:6–16.)

That is why Jesus came. He pulled back the veil. He showed the world what God really looked like—not a cold, condemning Judge but a warm, loving Father (solution to Problem Number One). And He offered to give them freedom from the laws' course and a new Spirit to guide them to truth (solution to Problem Number Two). That is why Paul could shout, ". . . where the Spirit of the Lord is, there is liberty [freedom]" (v. 17 KJV).

"Oh, no!" a believer might have answered. "There is that word *freedom* again. Freedom leaves you alone to decide what is right and what is wrong."

"Yes," Paul would have answered, "freedom lets you decide; but, no, freedom does not leave you alone to decide. The Spirit of the Lord is with you. Look to Him. Listen to Him. Talk to Him. Confess to Him. Complain to Him. Question Him.

Throughout his letters, Paul promised what God's Spirit could do: live in them (1 Corinthians 3:16), guide them (Galatians 5:16), teach them (Ephesians 1:17), pray for them (Romans 8:26), protect them (Ephesians 6:17), use them (1 Corinthians 12:7), shape them (2 Corinthians 3:18), give them power (Romans 15:19), make them into God's children (Romans 8:16), and raise them from the dead to life everlasting (Galatians 6:8).

To the church in Galatia, Paul described what the Spirit's presence could mean: ". . . love, joy, peace, patience, kindness, goodness, fidelity, gentleness, and self-control" (Galatians 5:22, 23).

To the believers in Corinth who struggled with the problem of sexual lust, Paul used his second letter to explain that, as the believer struggles with his freedom or as the brothers and sisters seek to know and do right, the Spirit shines brighter and clearer in the seeker's life. Little by little, as the Spirit shines on the believer, he or she is changed to look like God, to act like God, and to be more like God. "Through his Spirit," Paul concludes, "we are transfigured into his likeness" (*see* 2 Corinthians 3:18).

Control Your Actions

When Paul told the Corinthians that *where the Spirit of the Lord is, there is freedom,* they responded with a familiar question. "Does this mean," they asked, "that we can do anything we want?" In reply to that question, Paul gave them three other questions they should ask, as guidelines for their new Christian freedom.

" 'I am free to do anything,' you say," he echoed them. "Yes, but not everything is for my good. No doubt I am free to do anything, but I for one will not let anything make free with me [be overpowered by any of them]" (1 Corinthians 6:12). One question the believer in Corinth had to ask and answer about any sexual thought or act was: *Is this good or is this bad for me?*

Paul knew that every individual had a unique set of circumstances and gifts to consider. He refused to give them easy lists that would only prove inadequate and enslaving. So he made them wrestle with the hard question: "Will this sexual thought or act lead *me* to more health, more growth, more wholeness, and more freedom—or will it lead me to less health, less growth, less wholeness, and less freedom?"

Paul answers the Corinthian's next question with another question of his own: " 'We are free to do anything,' you say. Yes, but is everything good for us? 'We are free to do anything,' but does everything help the building of the community? Each of you must regard, not his own interests, but the other man's" (1 Corinthians 10:23, 24). So the second question a believer must ask and answer about any sexual thought or act was: *Is this good or is this bad for others?* Now the Christian's freedom to do anything he or she desires is made more complex. The believer is to consider the health, the growth, the wholeness, and the freedom of the other person, the family, the neighborhood, the whole world, and the church—in Corinth or around the globe.

He answers their next question: " 'What?' you say, 'is my freedom to be called in question by another man's conscience?' " (*see* v. 29). Paul not only leaves them on the horns of that dilemma but introduces yet another guideline for judging any sexual thought or act: ". . . whatever you are doing, do all for the honour of God" (1 Corinthians 10:31). A third question a believer must ask and answer about any sexual thought or act is: *Is this honoring to God? Will it give Him satisfaction? Will it please Him? Will it make others respect and honor God?*

I wonder if the readers of Paul's letter remembered Jesus' words as they scratched their heads in wonder at the difficult and demanding side of their new freedom? For Jesus Himself was the first to raise these three questions with His command: "Love the Lord your God with all your heart and love your neighbor as you love yourself."

Control Your Thoughts

Paul knew that sexual lust begins in a person's head. He instructed the believers in Corinth to cleanse themselves "from all that can defile flesh or spirit" (*see* 2 Corinthians 7:1). If the Christians asked, "How can we know for sure what is good and what is bad?" Paul answered, "A man gifted with the Spirit can judge the worth of everything . . ." (1 Corinthians 2:15). "We possess the mind of Christ," he reminded them in the next verse.

Again, Paul helped them understand the two-sided nature of Christian freedom. They had to judge. They had to decide. They had to think for themselves, but the Spirit was within them, helping them in every choice. The problem would come when believers quit struggling to know the mind of Christ and gave way, a little at a time, to unhealthy and destructive thoughts. Remember, Paul warned them of the end of that process: ". . . your thoughts may be corrupted and you may lose your single-hearted devotion to Christ" (2 Corinthians 11:3).

Paul told them stories about the children of Israel who stopped trying to think and obey the thoughts of God. They thought about their beautiful pagan neighbors instead. Eventually their lustful thoughts led them into lustful acts and even into worshiping pagan gods. Their bones lay in the desert because they let their evil thoughts guide them off the trail and away from the others whom God was leading. Paul reminded them: "These things happened as symbols to warn us not to set our desires on evil things, as they did" (1 Corinthians 10:6).

Choose Your Friends Carefully

"Make no mistake," Paul warned them, " 'Bad company is the ruin of a good character' " (1 Corinthians 15:33). Although Paul advised the new believers in Corinth not to marry unbelievers (2 Corinthians 6:14), it was not their personal contacts with non-Christians that bothered Paul most about the Corinthians. He said to them:

> In my letter I wrote that you must have nothing to do with [the immoral]. I was not, of course, referring to pagans . . . . To avoid them you would have to get out of the world altogether. I now write that you must have nothing to do with any so-called Christian who leads a loose life . . . . What business of mine is it to judge outsiders? God is their judge. You are judges within the fellowship . . . .
>
> 1 Corinthians 5:9–13

This is a dangerous piece of advice. But isn't freedom always dangerous? Of course Paul took a risk when he asked them to be careful of close friendships with believers who could mislead them. Of course he knew the danger of concluding this passage with the advice that they root out evil-doers from their midst. But in the same letter he gave specific guidelines to be considered before any unloving act of judgment. Read them all in 1 Corinthians 13.

> Love is patient; love is kind and envies no one. Love is never boastful, nor conceited, nor rude; never selfish, not quick to take offence. Love keeps no score of wrongs; does not gloat over other men's sins, but delights in the truth. There is nothing love cannot face; there is no limit to its faith, its hope, and its endurance.
>
> 1 Corinthians 13:4–7

Again Paul trusted them with both sides of Christian freedom. "Be on your guard," he warned them, "against the Christian who would lead you astray." Discipline your friendships. At the same time, let Christian love be your guide.

Surely this self-control that Paul ordered seemed difficult for the new believers. They must have been awed by all that he expected of them. The apostle's goal in life seemed simple on the one hand, but so complex on the other. "We therefore make it our ambition," he wrote them, "wherever we are, here or there, to be acceptable to him" (2 Corinthians 5:9). Again Paul left them with a question—to ask and be answered—and not a pat list or set of commands to follow. And those of us who struggle with sexual lust are left with this same question: "Is my thought or action or friendship acceptable to God?" Paul reminded them: "Whatsoever things we do, we do all to the glory of God" (*see* 1 Corinthians 10:31 KJV).

Let the Community of Faith Assist You in Your Struggle

From Paul's first letter to them, the Corinthians must have pictured the church's role in sexual-lust cases as angry judge and ruthless jury. At first reading, it looked as though Paul meant for believers to stone or excommunicate the guilty. But in his follow-up letter Paul confessed that his earlier commands to consign the guilty man's body to Satan and root him out of their community were given to get the church to take the matter seriously (*see* 2 Corinthians 7:11).

Paul didn't mean for them to destroy the guilty man, but to save him *and* the church. He shouted his angry commands to wake them up and warn them. And it worked. The Corinthians held a church meeting, took the matter seriously, and applied the appropriate penalty to the guilty man. We have no record of the meeting or its decision. But we do know how happy their action made Paul.

"Something very different is called for now: you must forgive the offender and put heart into him; the man's sorrow must not be made so severe as to overwhelm him. I urge you therefore to assure him of your love for him by a formal act" (2 Corinthians 2:7, 8). Again Paul demonstrated both sides of Christian freedom: Deal seriously with sexual lust, then be the loving force to rebuild the guilty man to health and restore him to his place in the Christian community. When it's over, Paul advised, put on a Sunday-night supper in his honor and welcome the no-longer-guilty man back into all the privileges of the Christian fellowship.

Thus, both the judgment and the mercy of God were to be demonstrated by the Corinthian believers. Paul taught them that it is not enough to point out the man's sin. Nor is it enough to love him and overlook his sinfulness. The community of faith must apply God's judgment and His mercy to the person who struggles with sexual lust.

And though that is a difficult task, Paul added as encouragement for the believer:

> Praise be to the God . . . whose consolation never fails us! He comforts us in all our troubles, so that we in turn may be able to comfort others in any trouble of theirs and to share with them the consolation we ourselves receive from God.
>
> 2 Corinthians 1:3, 4

Don't Get Overconfident About Sexual Lust

Paul scolded the Corinthians: "Your self-satisfaction ill becomes you . . ." (1 Corinthians 5:6). He warned them: "If you feel sure that you are standing firm, beware! You may fall" (1 Corinthians 10:12). He gave them a practical suggestion with his advice: "Examine yourselves: are you living the life of faith? Put yourselves to the test . . ." (2 Corinthians 13:5). He must have jarred them awake with this announcement: "For we must all have our lives laid open before the tribunal of Christ, where each must receive what is due to him for his conduct in the body, good or bad" (2 Corinthians 5:10).

Don't Get Overfearful About Sexual Lust

Again Paul reminded them (and us) of the other side of Christian freedom. Paul promised: ". . . God keeps faith, and he will not allow you to be tested above your powers, but when the test comes he will at the same time provide a way out, by enabling you to sustain it" (1 Corinthians 10:13). He comforted them about failure: "When, however, we do fall under the Lord's judgement, he is disciplining us, to save us from being condemned with the rest of the world" (1 Corinthians 11:32). Paul assured them that they would be able to ". . . stand firm and immovable, and work for the Lord always . . . since you know that in the Lord your labour cannot be lost" (1 Corinthians 15:58).

Paul himself had recently barely escaped death at the hands of his enemies. He confessed to the Corinthians: "This was meant to teach us not to place reliance on ourselves, but on God who raises the dead. From such mortal peril God delivered us; and he will deliver us again, he on whom our hope is fixed" (2 Corinthians 1:9, 10).

No Easy Victory Promised

Paul's conversion may have been a three-ring miracle, complete with blinding lights and echoing voices, but God refused to give Paul any easy miracle for the struggle he waged in his body. There were no easy victories for Paul. There would be none for the Christians in Corinth.

Paul confessed to them that he had prayed for a miracle to cure a problem in his body:

> . . . I was given a sharp physical pain which came as Satan's messenger to bruise me; this was to save me from being unduly elated. Three times I begged the Lord to rid me of it, but his answer was: 'My grace is all you need; power comes to its full strength in weakness' . . . .
>
> 2 Corinthians 12:7–9

Paul wanted an easy victory for his struggle and God did not grant the apostle's request. Instead, so far as we know, Paul struggled with this physical problem all his life.

I have heard Paul's "thorn in the flesh" described as everything from gas or gout to homosexuality. The Corinthians must have been glad that they could not know the exact nature of his physical struggle. That way, the teen-ager with acne, the paraplegic, the emaciated old woman, the overweight single, the devout one facing martyrdom, or the person who struggled with sexual lust—*all* the believers—could hear God say again through Paul to them: *My grace is all you need.*

And Paul goes on to add his own response to God's re-fusal to grant him a quick and easy miracle for the struggle in his body:

> I shall therefore prefer to find my joy and pride in the
> very things that are my weakness; and then the power
> of Christ will come and rest upon me. Hence I am well
> content, for Christ's sake, with weakness, contempt,
> persecution, hardship, and frustration; for when I am
> weak, then I am strong.
>
>   2 Corinthians 12:9, 10

If there had been an easier answer to sexual lust than the Christians' struggle with freedom, I am sure Paul would have suggested it.

SUMMARY

Story 9: Paul and the Scandal in Corinth
(What New Testament Guidelines Are There to Follow?)

The Apostle Paul, founder and pastor of many first-century churches, wrote letters to his children in Christ throughout the Roman Empire. These letters give us invaluable insight into the practical, everyday side of the Christian's life.

When the church in Corinth seemed to ignore a case of sexual lust (incest) in one church family, Paul wrote two letters warning them to take sexual lust seriously. We comb these letters for Paul's clues to help us in our own struggle with sexual lust.

1. Paul saw life as warfare.
2. Christ has won the war.
3. But the battles go on.
4. Your body is a battlefield.
5. There are guidelines to help you in the battle.
6. Let the Holy Spirit help you win the battle.
7. Control your actions:
    "Is this good for me?"
    "Is this good for my neighbor?"
    "Does this honor God?"
8. Control your thoughts.
9. Choose your friends carefully.
10. Let the community of faith help you in your struggle.
11. Don't get overconfident about sexual lust.
12. Don't get overfearful about sexual lust.
13. There will be no easy victories.

1 and 2 Corinthians   Paul's Guidelines to the
                       Church in Corinth.

Story 10

A NIGHT ON THE ROAD
(How Can Paul's New Testament Guidelines
Really Help Me?)

Lyla double-parks our Volvo near the United Airlines
Terminal at Los Angeles International Airport. "I love
you," she shouts, pulling back into traffic. "I love you,
too," I answer, sprinting towards the terminal and down
the rainbow-colored concourse to Gate 72. "Smoking or
non-smoking?" mutters an agent. A computer belches out
my boarding pass. A stewardess welcomes me "to the
friendly skies."

The skies can be friendly when I am traveling with my
wife or children to some vacation spot, or when I am head-
ing home to them after another long trip somewhere. But
when I am leaving home on one more high-demand,
heavy-pressure assignment, the skies can be very un-
friendly. The doors seal shut. The ramp glides away. I am
cut off from family and friends and surrounded by strangers. For five hours I will be strapped into Seat 24F. I can
never sit in one place very long, and what goes on in my
head is sometimes very hard to deal with.

Before we reach the end of the runway I have my date-
book out to list the items to be accomplished in the next ten
days. *Pressure:* I picture a stream of people expecting me to
perform and to produce brilliantly. *Guilt:* "Why do you

have to go this time, Daddy?'' *Anxiety:* Aren't I breathing awfully hard from that short run to catch the plane? *Loneliness:* Who are all these strangers? *Anger:* And where are all my friends when I need them? *Frustration:* Will I ever break out of this self-imposed, heavy-pressure, high-demand cycle?

We are ten thousand feet over the Pacific, turning towards the east. My foldaway table is covered with work, but I don't feel like working. I feel like talking to my wife, but we barely had time to say good-bye. I wish there were someone who could understand the crazy jumble of thoughts running through my head. I want to laugh. I want to waste time. I want someone to love me without putting any demands on that love; but I am alone or surrounded by strangers.

Two miles below me the sea sparkles in the early-morning sunlight and I think about God again. There *is* Someone who loves me without putting any demands on that love. I am not alone. "Thank You, Lord . . . ." My prayer may trail off after a few sentences, crowded out by static in my brain. Sometimes it is hard to pray, even when you are a professional at it. I carry a well-used Bible in my briefcase, but sometimes when I try to read it my attention span is thirty seconds long.

A steward interrupts to ask me my final destination. I could say, "New York's Kennedy Airport." Instead I answer, "The Promised Land." He grins and shakes his head in disbelief. I know many of the other 270 passengers would also grin and shake their heads in disbelief if they could know what I am thinking. But if Abraham or Moses or Samson were on board, if David or Solomon or Paul were my fellow passengers, they would understand. I know my weaknesses. I can read my symptoms. This 747 with its microwave ovens and deep recliner seats—and the Hyatt Regency with its indoor pool, plush rooms, and restaurants—will be my wilderness in the next few days.

My travel agent thinks it's just another business trip. But I know this journey could become another leg on my trip through temptation to the Promised Land. The stewardess thinks I am traveling alone. But I know the Spirit of God travels with me. The pilot's voice assures me of my safety and comfort. But I know that, unless I take the Apostle Paul's warning seriously, I could lose a battle to evil in the coming nights on the road.

Life Is Warfare

In the first century the Apostle Paul said that life is warfare. In 1976 a terrorist bomb exploded just outside a crowded restaurant in Jerusalem, just as my camera crew and I approached the place for dinner. Earlier that summer in England, I entered an underground train station minutes after another terrorist bomb had exploded, killing and maiming unsuspecting travelers. I had read about the invisible wars of terror, but it didn't make much difference to the way I lived until I saw the death and the destruction with my own eyes. Then every unattended suitcase, every airport locker, or every overparked car made me walk a little faster and feel a little more afraid. When I confessed my fear to a travel agent, she advised me, "Stay scared, Lovey. It may save your life."

This morning, as I pass through the airport security check, it is easy to be reminded of that war of terror, which an unseen enemy wages against my body. But I let those airport security police who frisk me and those girls in blue uniforms who X-ray my baggage remind me of the other war of terror that evil wages to maim my soul. I am tired, off guard, and feeling very unreligious. I am pressured, and my needs for "love without demand" are obvious. I am vulnerable. And sexual lust is only one of the many tactics which evil will use to terrorize me on this journey—if I will let it happen.

Now is the time the biblical guidelines can make all the difference. Now is the time I need to focus on God's great love for me and His guarantee to see me through my journey. Since the battle against temptation is waged in my head, Paul's biblical guidelines against temptation have become more helpful to me when I ask them as questions. These questions are not unlike the airport security system. They help me search out signs of evil and maintain vigilance over my soul.

The seat-belt sign flashes off. We are somewhere above the California desert. It is time to ask the first of my security-check questions:

> Do I really believe that there is a war being waged this moment between God and Satan for my soul?

The stewardess delivers coffee with the morning *Los Angeles Times*. The lead story is one illustration that Paul's warning is to be taken seriously. Life is warfare, and the headlines—INCEST IS EPIDEMIC IN AMERICA—demonstrate it. A father rapes his teenage daughter after giving her a massage which the family doctor has prescribed. Two brothers, aged fourteen and twelve, confess to forcing their ten-year-old sister to have sexual intercourse with them since she was six. A young girl is seduced and sexually assaulted more than fifty times by her grandfather and her uncle and then is blamed by her parents for what has happened. A teenage boy sodomizes his younger brother after watching a pornographic film.

The news story illustrates in lurid detail the problem of incest in America. The average victim is eleven years old. The long-range effects on those innocent young victims are horrendous. And those who commit incest are often "normal," hard-working, otherwise law-abiding citizens. They live in our neighborhoods. They work and worship beside us. They read the headlines that we read and turn away in shock and disgust, never dreaming that one day they will read their own names in those same, ugly headlines.

This story of incest is only one of the many variations of sexual lust in the headlines that help me take the Bible's warning seriously. Who needs more proof that evil is a silent, invisible enemy who stalks every one of us and works day and night to do us in? When ancient Bible stories or modern headlines do not convince me, I think about my own experience. I am no longer surprised by the variety of ugly, destructive thoughts that can appear without invitation in my brain. I am convinced that, given the wrong set of circumstances, these awful headlines (or their like) could one day have my name in them, too. So, at the beginning of this trip it is easy to answer, "Yes! There is a war being waged this moment between God and Satan for my soul!"

Christ Has Won the War

I will be thousands of miles away from my home and family for the next ten days. In New York I will live within easy distance of endless opportunities for sexual lust. I know how vulnerable I can be to lust, given the right situation. But before I get nervous, it is time to ask another security-check question:

> Do I really believe that God has won the war for me in the life and death and resurrection of Jesus?

Even as I read the tragic headlines and remind myself to stay alert, I can look the Evil One in the eye and say, "I do not need to be afraid of you anymore." This is the other side, the good news. Of course it is difficult to understand how Jesus' death on a cross two thousand years ago can pardon me before God of my past and future failures. But the Bible says it is true, and because I believe that good news, it makes all the difference in my immediate struggle with sexual lust.

In airplanes and airports, hotel rooms and restaurants, I will fight a battle in the war that has already been won for me. Whether I win or lose the battle in New York, I am a winner in God's eyes. Because of His incredible love for me, I don't have to be afraid of my past or my future anymore.

I have sung about this amazing grace all my life, but I must confess that I have had trouble believing it when it comes to my sexual lust. The cycle is all too clear in me. I set a high goal. Sometimes I reach it. Other times I fail. When I fail, I try again. And if I fail again, Satan laughs at me and whispers, "You aren't making it, Mel." Doubt and guilt and failure try to drag me down. I let the question remind me that God has won this war already. I don't have to win it. Christ has won it for me. All He asks is that I try. And while I am trying, if I fail, He will forgive me and love me all the same. In the process I will grow stronger and more sure of His grace. Even when I am stumbling about, He is teaching me and guiding me and loving me. Whatever happens, I can be sure that God can use it for my good. Somewhere over the Rockies I am humming "Amazing Grace." I will hum it a lot before this trip is over.

The Battle Goes On

Now the irony continues. Though God has won the war, the battle goes on. I think of the apostle's own struggle to keep his body disciplined and in control, ". . . for fear that after preaching to others I should find myself rejected" (1 Corinthians 9:27). It is difficult to maintain a healthy tension between what I need to do and what God has already done for me. But I see it as a lifelong adventure.

This 747 jumbo jet has logged 400,000 accident-free air miles. Yet nothing is taken for granted. The mechanics and the crew put the airplane through a rigorous preflight safety check. At every point in our journey the pilot will keep close watch on dials, gauges, computer readouts, and blinking warning lights. No one calls the pilot "paranoid" because he stays alert to danger. Why should my approach to life be any different?

Like the pilot alert to save his aircraft from disaster, I will keep watch over my soul. Evil never sleeps. Of course, this sounds melodramatic. My culture grins and calls me to relax and take all the gusto I can get. But Paul has reminded me to stay on guard. Satan wages war against my soul around the clock. God has won the war for me, but the battles never stop.

As the giant airliner makes its final descent into New York, the crew is alert to every possible danger. I, too, am preparing for the next stage in my journey by asking this question:

> Where will evil attack me next, and what should I do about it?

I know my limits. I am tired, off guard, and excited. I am far from home and family. My clock is off, and when everybody should be sleeping I will lie lonely and bored on my hotel bed. Warning lights blink on.

It is obvious where evil might launch its next attack. Now what should I do to keep from becoming its victim? The hotel pool closes at 10:00 P.M. I will take a swim and then call Lyla. To talk awhile will help us both. Then I will read from *Psalms Now* and watch a late-night talk show. The night will pass. Eventually I will sleep. In the morning friends will meet me and life will seem normal again.

Paul promised me: ". . . when the test comes [God] will at the same time provide a way out, by enabling you to sustain it" (1 Corinthians 10:13). I trust God for that "way out," but I figure it can only help if I know my limits and work out my own little plan to stay safely within them.

My Body Is a Battlefield

Leaving the terminal for my hotel, I am still whistling "Amazing Grace" and feeling terribly confident about winning the battle in my body, when suddenly it begins again. Riding in the limousine I find myself stimulated by a beautiful body sitting across the aisle. Later, in the spectacular hotel lobby, my eyes, ears, and nose attract me to sensual shapes and sounds and smells of other beautiful bodies that surround me. Automatically, my glands, muscles, nerve endings, and brain respond. The battle is on.

Don't misunderstand me. I am glad I have a body. Just because I agree with the Apostle Paul that my body is a battlefield, I am not saying that my body is bad, or that I don't like mine, or that it is wrong to be sexually aroused by someone else's body.

Quite the opposite is true. Our bodies and their sexuality are a gift from God. We are sexual beings all day, every day of our lives. We relate to each other sexually. It is normal to be attracted to each other's bodies. We communicate with each other through our "body language." We bring joy and comfort and aid to each other through our bodies. In countless ways we relate to each other through our bodies, and sex is always there, influencing those relationships. There is no way we should (or could) stop the full-time role which sexuality plays in our bodies. God wants me to be a sexual being. He wants me to enjoy my body, to be grateful for it, and to understand and control it better.

After a hot shower, I stand in front of the hotel bathroom's full-length mirror, looking at my God-given body. I marvel at its mystery and at its power to support and sustain me. And I thank God for it:

Thank You, Father, for my body. I confess there are things about it I would like to change. But You have lovingly created me. You have a purpose and a plan for my body with all its mystery. When I am tempted to misuse my body, deliver me. When I am sexually tested, make me strong. For my body— its pleasure, its pain, and its amazing promise—I give You thanks!

I could pray longer, but I'm naked and freezing cold. Besides, it's time to ask a question I struggle with the most. Try it yourself. Take off your clothes—right now (unless you're reading this in an airport waiting room or religious bookstore). Get in a comfortable, private place. Look at yourself in a mirror. Thank God for your body and its sexuality. Then ask the next question I ask myself:

Will I control my body today—or will I let my body control me?

Guidelines to Help in Battle

Later, the glass-and-chrome elevator delivers me noiselessly into a world of easy lust in the hotel's plush leather lobby, gourmet restaurants, cozy drinking establishments, and fully-stocked liquor and magazine stores. Curbside taxi drivers promise skin flicks, massage parlors, night spots, and dating services—or "Whatever turns you on, Buddy." Even in the coffee shop where I settle for a sandwich before my swim, another lonely body smiles and gestures casually from across the room.

Here I am neither husband nor father, pastor nor professor. I am one more anonymous body in a crowd of other lonely, anonymous bodies. Upstairs in front of the mirror, it was easy to decide that I would control my body, but down here the battle gets more complex.

It is not always easy to know what is right or wrong about sexual behavior. We want specific rules to guide us. So we rush to our Bibles, our pastors, or our heroes to find new laws that tell us what we can or cannot do. When we find a rule, no matter how obscure or out of context, we quote it with relief. Then we disobey it anyway. It's the old Pharisees' game, and we love to play it. We prefer censorship to self-control. We prefer the old laws to the new Christian freedom. The trouble is that for every specific law we uncover, there will be a dozen choices left for us to make anyway. Look at the Corinthians' dilemma.

Paul gave them only the sketchiest outline of sexual acts he considered off-limits: incest, adultery, sodomy, and prostitution. It is also apparent that both Jesus and Paul taught that sexual intercourse was meant for marriage. After that, the new believers had to make sexual decisions for themselves.

Paul didn't attempt to give specific rules to the single person who wanted to get married but could not find a mate. He didn't offer laws to govern the questions of masturbation, birth control, Corinthian massage parlors, or pornographic wall paintings. He didn't solve the problem of those who from childhood have strong sexual desire only for persons of their own sex—or people who want their sex changed surgically. He didn't even allude to the mentally or emotionally retarded who have normal sex drives and no "acceptable" way to meet them—or the handicapped person whose misshapen body prevents "normal" sexual intercourse. Paul didn't mention kissing or petting, tight togas, X-rated Greek plays, or young couples in love and about to be married, who want to make love the night before their wedding. There were no adequate instructions for every sexual choice—to guide Corinthian businessmen overnight in Athens on business.

Like all the Bible authors, Paul was not specific in answering every sexual question. But he did tell us who is to be responsible for making the decisions: ". . . each one must order his life according to the gift the Lord has granted him and his condition when God called him" (1 Corinthians 7:17).

This week as I wander anonymously through a world of easy sexual lust, I will ask myself first:

> Does the Bible give me a clear warning against this specific sexual thought or act?

If so, I will try to obey that warning. If there is no specific biblical command, I will do my best to consider the great Old Testament stories, the wisdom of ancient kings and prophets, the New Testament letters, and the life and teachings of Jesus. These will answer this alternate question:

> What general biblical guidelines are there
> to help me make my own responsible decision?

Let the Holy Spirit Help

I am in New York City now. When my defenses are down, the Big Apple works on me like that "little apple" in Eden worked on Adam and Eve. I get turned on by the sensual, nighttime lure of Times Square, Broadway, Greenwich Village, and the ethnic neighborhoods with shops that never close and lights that always flicker a welcome.

The first day's conference has recessed for a long lunch break. So this California boy grabs a subway to Wall Street's Trinity Church. I love to sit in a rear pew of this historic old chapel and listen to the organist practice a prelude and fugue while I read the Word and pray. It is my best daytime defense against New York's lure at night.

Remember the prophet Hosea's advice? His solution for Israel's idolatry and sexual lust was in knowing God. To know God, summarized the prophet, is to obey Him, to love Him, and to fellowship with Him forever. As one frequently tempted, I spend a lot of time working to know God better. I have found no greater help in my struggle against sexual lust than staying alive to the Spirit of God in my life. That's why I ask myself continually:

> What have I done today to know God better?

Bonhoeffer advised his students in *Life Together:* "Let the first thought and the first word of every day belong to God." In my hotel room before I roll out of bed, I thank God for the new day and ask Him to guide me in it. In the shower I pray for my wife and family and friends. Before breakfast I try to read a Psalm and memorize a line or two of it. During the day, I play a secret game of looking for spiritual truths in secular billboards and advertisements. (For example, think about the Pan American Airlines ad: "All of us come from someplace else." Or Seagram's V.O. whisky's bold reminder: "There are signs that tell you where to go and how to go.") All day long I keep a running dialogue with God's Spirit in my head: "Guide me, Lord, Teach me. Show me Your way."

I am not alone in my struggle with sexual lust. God's Spirit is always with me, loving me, guiding me, forgiving me, and shaping me into His son. These questions I ask are not asked into empty space, but asked of God—who hears them, answers them, and changes me by His presence from what I am to what He dreams for me to be.

Control Your Thoughts and Actions

For the past six days I have been cooped up in conference rooms and hotel coffee shops. My wife is three thousand miles away. Cold showers and long-distance phone calls aren't helping much, and I am up to a hundred laps in the hotel pool. Why shouldn't I take advantage of New York's many ways to relieve my sexual pressure? No one knows me here. It could be my little secret. I am free to fantasize and even act out those fantasies.

And the Apostle Paul's words echo across the centuries: "Yes, you are free to do anything, but not everything is for your good" (*see* 1 Corinthians 6:12). So, as I wander around the city, feeling bored and restless, the Holy Spirit guides me through the question:

> Is this good for me?

The evening's work session is over. I am walking through Times Square. I enter a busy bookstore to browse. I admit I should have asked the question "Is this good for me?" before this moment. I didn't. I was tired and off guard. I left the hotel and entered this store without thinking. Now I have wandered from the hardback philosophy-and-religion section to a wall of colorful magazines and paperbacks that really get my fantasies flowing.

One sure result of tiredness or boredom or anxiety is a quick sexual lust in the head. Sure, anyone can buy a *Playboy* magazine, or just look at a nearby beautiful body, or sit back and picture a body that turns you on (in this case, I don't mean your spouse), and let your fantasies soar.

There is a problem, however. Jesus warned us that sexual lust in our heads can be as harmful as the lustful sexual act (*see* Matthew 5:27, 28). Paul warned the Corinthians that fantasies of sexual lust can be destructive (*see* 1 Corinthians 10:6). He told them some frightening stories to make his point. We have proof of our own: the Manson family, Richard Speck, the Boston Strangler, Jack the Ripper, and perhaps the more recent Son of Sam. The errant children of Israel and you and I are all the same in that sexual lust begins in the brain.

Sexual fantasies are not all evil. A healthy, normal, creative sexual thought life can be good and necessary when part of the framework of marriage. But sexual fantasies can also be the beginning of sexual lust. There is no moment like *this* moment to begin controlling those fantasies which are destructive, difficult to handle, and dehumanizing. You are the one to judge which sexual fantasies are right and helpful and which cause you guilt or fear or arouse sexual lust. You are the only one who can and must control them.

Finally, in the Times Square bookstore, the question gets through to me—"Is this good for me?" Are these sexy, provocative books and magazines helping my current struggle with sexual lust? Should I even be in this bookstore (let alone in Times Square) in my present state of mind?

The question helps even more when followed by: "What *would* be good for me, then?" The meetings are boring. I deserve time off. What could I do to combat my boredom creatively and reward myself for the past six days of hard work? My friends Ken and Jane Medema live just through the Holland Tunnel. I call them. They invite me to their home. In thirty minutes I am with them. We are laughing hilariously at how quickly I became "a dirty old man" and we are thanking God for His loving sustaining presence in our lives.

It is Jane who reminds me of the other question I should have asked before wandering into Times Square that night. Jesus knew that if we only considered *ourselves* in making our decisions, it would be disastrous. He said, "Love your neighbor as you love yourself." Jane said, "While you were lechering about the sexual-lust capital of the world, did you think about your wife and what was good for her in that moment?" Paul made it clear to the Corinthians that there is a second question to consider before any decision is made:

Is this good for others?

How easy it is to forget to ask how my sexual lust might affect my wife, my children, my friends, my associates, my parents, and all those who have invested their lives in me or who look to me as an example. What could be the long-range effects of my sexual lust on them? Yielding to sexual temptation is a betrayal of their trust and confidence, and—in the case of my wife and children—a violation of the marriage covenant which is a basis of the family unit.

But it is also easy to forget to ask how one's sexual thoughts or behavior affect persons even more directly involved. Innocent children who are enticed or forced into sexual relations bear the emotional scars for the rest of their lives. The older youth or adult who is used to satisfy sexual lust may seem less affected than a child, but there are no guarantees. The long-range suffering which one's lust may cause for others is not worth the risk one takes. As Christians, we *are* our brothers' (and our sisters') keepers, and all our thoughts and actions should be viewed in the light of what is good for them.

Of course, there is yet a third question that I should have asked in Times Square:

> Does this honor God?

Paul said, "Honor God in your body" (*see* 1 Corinthians 6:20). In the early-morning hours, the taxi delivers me back to my hotel after an unforgettable evening with my brother and sister in Christ. In my room I remember how easy it would have been that night in Times Square to give in to sexual lust.

How quickly I forgot how God sees my body. First, His Spirit lives within my body. Second, my body is the body of Christ, commissioned to do His work in the world. Third,

God loves my body. He died to rescue it and will one day raise it from the grave. And yet, in one night of boredom and sexual pressure, I could have thrown that all away.

Lying in bed, I think about God's dreams for my body. I want to honor Him with my thoughts and with my acts. I want to use my body in His service. And one day when my struggle is over, I want Him to reach out across eternity and take me in His arms in a great, loving hug of celebration while the heavens echo with His happy words: "Well done, struggler. Well done!"

Control Your Friendships

By the way, I also have a Christian friend in New York whom I am glad I did not call last night. This morning in the airport as I wait for TWA's Flight 97 back to Los Angeles, I can't help thinking what might have happened if I had called that person instead of Ken and Jane. Let's face it, since childhood we have been warned against the bad influence which nonbelievers may have on our lives. But who ever warned us about the bad influence we believers can have on each other?

Paul was not half so afraid of the pagans' influence on the Christian's life, as he was afraid of the believers' influence on each other. "What business of mine is it to judge outsiders?" Paul asked them. "God is their judge. You are judges within the fellowship . . ." (1 Corinthians 5:12, 13). That single piece of advice could save us from the serious mistakes we make in our attempts to decide what is right or wrong for our pagan neighbors. Rather, we should be assisting one another with the rampant sexual lust within the church.

You may have heard stories about organists who run off with pastors, deacons who have affairs with choir members, and youth leaders who "get someone in trouble" at camp. Christians relate to each other in their maleness or femaleness the same as everybody else. It is good and right and normal to be attracted to each other's bodies, as well as each other's minds. We cannot or should not eliminate each other's sexuality. The problem begins when our sexuality doesn't just influence our relationships but begins to take power over them.

I am sexually aware of several of my Christian friends and acquaintances. It is a normal and appropriate reaction. But I know how quickly a normal sexual response can become sexual lust. I know how subtly evil enters into the purest relationship, and how quickly sexual teasing and humor can lead to seduction and sexual lust. Paul said to be on guard against lust within the community. So I ask myself:

> Will my proximity to this person at this time
> lead us both to health and wholeness or to sexual lust?

To discipline and control Christian friendships is a difficult and demanding task for me. When I am weak or sexually vulnerable or far from home and family, there are certain Christian friends I avoid—not because I don't want to be around them, but because I know my temptation limits and want to stay within them.

Let the Community Help You

Ken and Jane Medema are my brother and sister in Christ. They are only two of the many members of the body of Christ around the world to whom I can turn in times of crisis. I have confessed my weaknesses to them. I can trust them to drop what they are doing and come to my aid when

I need them. I don't have to fake the Christian smile or mutter, "I'm fine," when they ask me how I am doing. If I am struggling with *any* spiritual battle, I can trust them to come through for me.

Evil wants me to struggle alone. Evil wants me to go on faking it. Evil wants me to think that my struggle with sexual lust or other temptation is unique and that no one would understand. Evil wants me to be afraid to trust the Christian community. But evil is wrong.

Two thousand years ago the Holy Spirit came to build Christ's body, the church. My brothers and sisters in that body are His gift to me. I never have to struggle alone again. That is why when I am feeling lonely in the battle I ask:

> Who is there in the body of Christ who could hear my confession, understand my dilemma, pray with me, and share my burden?

Whether God leads you to a brother or sister with professional counseling skills or a Christian stranger or a longtime friend, let the community help you in your struggle. My brothers and sisters in Christ have made all the difference for me.

No Easy Victory

The pilot says we are 18,000 feet above Death Valley on our final descent to Los Angeles International Airport. Somewhere on the freeway, Lyla is steering our Volvo through the traffic. In minutes I will grab my suitcase and run through the crowded concourse to the street where she is double-parked. I will lean through the window and kiss her while a voice mutters, "No parking, please," and the officer motions angrily. And together we will drive home again.

But right now I am thinking about that black-toupeed, tuxedo-jacketed television healer I mentioned at the beginning of this book as saying, "Praise God! Someone out there in videoland has been healed of sexual lust." How mad it made me when I heard him say it! I have been a Christian since my childhood. I have experienced the love and the power and the forgiveness of God in my daily struggles as I try to walk His path. I am constantly amazed and excited by what the Holy Spirit is doing in my life and in the lives of others like me. I don't doubt for a minute God's ability and willingness to grant miraculous deliverance from sexual lust, too. I believe in miracles. But something about the evangelist-healer's words make me angry and uncomfortable still.

Perhaps I am tasting sour grapes because God hasn't "healed me of sexual lust" like the healing "out there in videoland." Perhaps I am growing jaded from the glut of Christian books and talk shows and motion pictures which feature believers who were born again and never seem to struggle with anything after that, especially sexual lust. Or perhaps it is because the currently popular, happy-ever-after versions of the Christian faith are so unlike Christian truth as I understand and experience it. Whatever the reason for my anger and discomfort, I am convinced that Scripture calls us *not* to easy miracles but to the joyful, hopeful, confident struggle with our own Christian freedom. That's what leads me to this last question:

Am I still looking for an easy miracle, or am I willing to trust God in my lifelong struggle with temptation?

Ten years ago, I could not have written these words. Like Paul, I was too busy praying for a miracle. I hoped that God would rescue me once and for all from my battles with sexual lust. But God has not given me that big miracle. Instead He has given me little miracles all along the way—as He has with all my struggles.

When I was guilty of giving in to temptation, He gave me the miracle of Jesus on the cross to clear me of the guilt forever. When I felt perplexed, He gave me the miracle of His Word to guide me. When I felt I would never win, He gave me the miracle of His Spirit who is gradually shaping me into a winner. When I needed people to love me, to comfort me, to forgive me, He gave me the miracle of His body, the church: my wife and children, counselors, friends, parents, pastors, teachers. When I felt trapped by laws, He gave me Christian freedom and said, "Use your head. Make decisions. Trust Me!" When I failed, He gave me the miracle of His forgiveness.

Maybe that's what the television healer meant when he said, "Praise God! Someone out there in videoland has been healed of sexual lust." Maybe he meant me.

I *have* been healed of sexual lust. Yet my struggle with temptation goes on. My human struggle will never end. For struggle is part of God's plan to shape and use my life. All my struggles have been a way for Him to teach me to depend on Him and on His community. Now, in a moment of weakness, when I still pray for miracles, God answers me as He once answered Paul: ". . . My grace is all you need; power comes to its full strength in weakness" (2 Corinthians 12:9). After years of struggle, I am finding it easier to respond in Paul's words:

I shall therefore prefer to find my joy and pride in the very things that are my weakness; and then the power of Christ will come and rest upon me. Hence I am well content, for Christ's sake, with weakness . . . for when I am weak, then I am strong.

2 Corinthians 12:10

SUMMARY

Story 10: A Night on the Road

(How Can Paul's New Testament Guidelines Really Help Me?)

1. Do I really believe there is a war being waged this moment between God and Satan for my soul?

2. Do I really believe that God has won that war for me in the life and death and resurrection of Jesus?

3. Where will evil attack me next, and what should I do about it?

4. Will I control my body today, or will I let my body control me?

5. Does the Bible give me a clear warning against this specific sexual thought or act?

6. If there are no specific warnings, what general biblical guidelines are there to help me make my own responsible decision?

7. What have I done today to know God better?

8. Before I decide, I ask:
   "Is this good for me?"
   "Is this good for others?"
   "Does this honor God?"

9. Will my proximity to this person at this time lead us both to health and wholeness—or to sexual lust?

10. Who is there in the body of Christ who could hear my confession, understand my problem, pray with me, and share my burden?

11. Am I still looking for an easy miracle, or am I willing to trust God in my lifelong struggle with temptation?